"One of the biggest challenges of our fast changing world is how to prepare our children adequately for their future. This timely book addresses why, what and how education can become relevant for children around the world. Professor Reimers and his colleagues discuss how education systems have changed in the past as well as the challenges and opportunities that lie ahead for teachers, students and schools as the world learns to cope with the demands of the twenty first century."

Rukmini Banerji, CEO, Pratham

"There's no more critical question facing today's educators and policymakers than how we can reimagine education at scale so that the children growing up today gain the competencies, mindsets, values, awareness, and agency to shape a better future for themselves and all of us. Fernando Reimers has given us a huge gift with his thoughtful introduction and this compendium of thoughts from practitioners around the world who are on the forefront of grappling with this challenge. This is a treasure trove of invaluable insights that can help us all succeed in this pursuit which is so crucial for our collective welfare."

Wendy Kopp, CEO & Co-founder, Teach For All

"This book is an invaluable guide to policy makers, educational leaders, practitioners and researchers concerned with scaling up 21st century education. How can educational systems around the world ensure that schools are equipping students with highly relevant competencies to function in rapidly changing contexts? Drawing on his encyclopedic knowledge of education reform history, global leadership in educational innovation and deep involvement in educational communities across continents, Fernando Reimers' insights shed an unfamiliar light on some of our current understanding of scalable change in education. Unlike efficiency changes pertaining to creating opportunities for schooling or enhancing the core of teaching and learning we are desperately in need of understanding the process of scaling up education for relevance – where learners are truly

D0424784

empowered with the desired competencies to learn to learn, to ride on technologies as intelligent assists to human creativity and to be contributing global citizens. Through this publication Fernando invites us into this journey and process of accelerating the enhancement of reform for 21st century relevancy and impact by understanding with humility a new purposeful learning orientation, and facilitating sustainable consensus where " why" convictions are translated into how in authentic standards, norms and practices. The book also enlightens us on the importance of anchoring on local contexts while being responsive to technological changes, social changes and today's personalization of education."

Professor Tan Oon Seng, Nanyang Technological University, Singapore

"This book is a timely compilation of the lessons learned by a group of educators from various countries leading efforts to bring to scale approaches to educate the whole child. The acceleration of political, economic and social changes demands that we face the question of how best to educate the young for an uncertain future with urgency and determination, and the answers to such questions are likely to come from the collaboration among researchers, practitioners and policy makers illustrated by the contributors to this volume."

James E. Ryan, Dean of the Faculty and Charles William Eliot Professor, Harvard Graduate School of Education

"Education that responds to the needs of all 21st Century learners is not only a desirable goal, but an ethical imperative. Indeed, this is precisely the focus of our Sustainable Development Goal 4-Education 2030 agenda, which calls for 'inclusive and equitable education and lifelong learning for all'. Realizing this transformative vision means empowering all learners to be able to face the myriad challenges ahead of them.

Are our schools responding to these challenges with education that is relevant to the needs of our learners? The answer suggested by Professor Fernando M. Reimers and other global leaders in education gives us a reason for optimism: yes, remarkable advances are taking place throughout the world; the challenge now is to ensure that such innovations are the rule rather than the exception. I heartily recommend "Empowering All Students At Scale", a valuable resource offering inspiration and insights for policy-makers and other leaders looking to bring such advances to scale for the benefit of all learners."

Gwang-Jo Kim, Director, UNESCO Asia Pacific Regional Bureau for Education"

"This excellent publication draws from the exchange of views and collaboration among researchers and policymakers on scaling up innovative approaches to building XXIst century skills in countries in different stages in their education improvement journey. I was happy and honored to have been part of this collective effort lead by Fernando Reimers during my time as visiting professor at Harvard.

Having been a policymaker myself, I find this possibility of collective learning unique, as it gave the opportunity for the participating countries to draw on the successes and failures of other geographies and thus be able to leapfrog education improvements. In a context of huge uncertainties in the world, where a growing need, emphasized in the book, of relevance-enhancing change in Education emerges, with all its difficulties of building and sustaining new consensus on what competencies need to be learned and how, this publication comes as an incredibly useful resource for all of us that are struggling to ensure quality and relevant education for all, especially for the most vulnerable kids in our countries."

Claudia Costin, Director of CEIPE- Center for Excellence and Innovation in Education Policies

Empowering All Students At Scale

Fernando M. Reimers (Editor)

With contributions from

Alejandro Almazan Zimerman, Connie K. Chung,
Allan J. Coutinho, Armando Estrada,
Luis E. Garcia de Brigard, Paulina Grino,
Santiago Isaza Arango, Ken Kay, Cesar Alberto Loeza
Altamirano, Charlie MacCormack, Eileen McGivney,
María Carolina Meza, María Figueroa, Felipe Martínez,
Pak Tee Ng, and Rafael C. P. Parente

ISBN-13: 978-1545486832

Library of Congress Control Number: 2017906111

Table of Contents

Making education for all relevant at scale

Fernando M. Reimers, Ford Foundation Professor of the Practice of International Education, Harvard Graduate School of Education

The world has, for some time now, been changing rapidly: technological change, demographic changes, economic changes, even climate changes. These transformations have caused some to be concerned that schools may not be adequately helping students to develop the competencies necessary to participate in society and to adequately address these changes. Expressive of such concern are views that argue that schools have not changed at all, or changed too little, since they were invented, or views arguing that schools are unable to sufficiently rapidly transform themselves, or to bring the necessary innovations to sufficient scale to help the majority of students gain the competencies that they will need in the future. By change at scale, I mean change in the nature of teaching and learning that is observed consistently across the majority of schools within a network—where membership in the network is defined by belonging to the same administrative jurisdiction—to a set of schools targeted by the same programmatic efforts of improvement, or to a set of schools that self-identify as sharing a particular set of goals and identity and commit to shared norms and practices.

These concerns about the paucity of educational innovation notwithstanding, there are plenty of examples of educational change around the world, often at significant scale. Not only have public schools succeeded in providing access to school to the majority of the world's children mostly over the last century, but school expansion and primary school completion in the developing world outperforms expansion in early industrialized countries, net of the differences in per capita income between nations, and average levels of schooling of the population in the developing world exceed the levels of education of the population early industrialized nations, at the historical point when levels of per capita income were comparable to those today in the developing world (Glewwe and Muralidharan, 2015). Such educational achievements would not have been possible without significant change in the institutions of education. Those who think schools have changed little over the last century overestimate what was learned in the first public schools invented in the mid nineteen century, their succees in enrolling all children and their efficiency in helping students complete the expected course of studies.

The concerns over the question of change at scale therefor stem not from the inability of schools to change, or even to change at scale, but from an insufficient understanding of the *process* through which schools change at scale and the consequent limitation in our capacity to manage their future evolution. The problem, therefore, is not with the capacity of school systems to change, the problem is with our capacity to make that change predictable and to manage it. Simply put, rather than decrying schools' inability to change, we need more understanding of how they do change at scale.

To advance our understanding of how schools change at scale, it is helpful to distinguish three forms of educational change: changes in the number and kind of students schools aim to serve; changes in instruction reflecting curricular goals on which there is wide consensus on goals as well as on the instructional practices to achieve such goals; and changes in instruction reflecting emerging notions of what competencies matter, but not widespread consensus on either goals or instructional practices to achieve them. Knowledge of how education systems change at scale is more developed for the first two forms of change, which I will call *efficiency enhancing change*, than for the third form of change, which I will call *relevancy enhancing change*. The paucity of knowledge of how to scale relevancy enhancing reforms is paradoxical given that there are ongoing efforts to scale such reforms, whether they have been successful or not. As a result, practitioners involved in these efforts know quite a bit about the barriers to scaling such efforts, as well as about the conditions which are necessary for success. It appears that in this case theory and research trail practice—that we know more than we think we do, or at least that those who lead those efforts know more than those who study them. This is a case of a mismatch between public and private knowledge.

Accelerating the process of knowing how to support relevancy enhancing reform requires making explicit and visible the private knowledge that has been gained by those who have attempted relevancy enhancing reforms at scale, and creating conditions that enable the formalization of such knowledge so that we can examine and test the hypotheses that emerge from such formalization. In other words, we need to make the private and tacit knowledge gained from the practice of educational change at scale public and visible, and therefore verifiable. This publication is an attempt to contribute to such process. It is the result of a two day think tank which brought together leaders of thought and practice from Brazil, Chile, China, Colombia, India, Mexico, Singapore, and the United States—all of whom are involved in leading efforts at scale to transform schools so that students can develop competencies which are relevant to the demands of the 21st century. I am very appreciative of all those who participated in the Think Tank, and especially of those who were able to write the reflections compiled in this book. I am also very grateful to Nell O'Donnell for her skilled editing of the submissions.

We convened this meeting as part of the work of the Global Education Innovation Initiative, a research and practice collaborative that seeks to understand and enhance the capacity of public education systems to provide students with effective opportunities to learn what they need to live fulfilling lives and to improve the world. The Global Education Innovation Initiative advances three inter-related sets of activities: applied research, education dialogues, and the development of frameworks and tools to support the consistent adoption of effective educational practices at scale. As part of our applied research work, we have completed a synthesis of research on competencies relevant in the 21st century, and used the report to then examine which of these competencies are addressed in the curriculum frameworks of several education systems (Reimers & Chung, 2016). We have also completed a study of various programs of teacher professional development to support pedagogies that provide a balanced education, addressing cognitive, emotional, and social domains. From those two studies we learned that there are numerous examples of education initiatives that provide a balanced 21st century education, but far fewer that have reached significant scale. It was this realization that motivated this think tank.

The education dialogues that are carried out as part of the Global Education Innovation Initiative bring together researchers, policy makers, and leaders of practice to foster learning across these groups for the purpose of advancing the translation of research into reform initiatives, or to translate knowledge gained from practice into researchable propositions. This approach is informed by work that highlights the importance of engaging education practitioners in creating knowledge for the improvement of education, such as the work of Tony Bryk and associates on improvement networks (Bryk et al., 2015); by the framework of Informed Dialogue to support collaborative work between education practitioners, policy makers and researchers (Reimers & McGinn, 1997); and by the concept of "adaptive leadership" developed by Ron Heifetz and colleagues, to describe ways to support collective action in domains on which there is no agreement on the definition of problems or solutions (Heifetz et al., 2004).

An example of one such dialogue carried out as part of the initiative was a convening of education leaders from Massachusetts together with education leaders from Singapore, to examine ways of preparation of teachers and school principals. The lessons learned in that exchange are reflected in a short publication designed to stimulate a broad dialogue among leaders of teacher education institutions and other key stakeholders in the field of teacher preparation and support in Massachusetts (Reimers & O'Donnell, 2016). The think tank we convened in October of 2016 to discuss the challenges of scaling 21st century education reforms was another dialogue of the Global Education Innovation Initiative. All participants in this think tank were invited to contribute reflections following the two-day meeting. This compilation was shared with all those who participated in the Think Tank who were invited to use this knowledge in developing country specific strategies to foster collective leadership efforts to advance 21st century education at scale in their respective jurisdictions. Those plans were then presented and received feedback at a global conference convened by the Global Education Innovation Initiative in May of 2017 which brought together over 200 leaders of thought and practice involved in relevance enhancing reform efforts. This iterative process that supports educational transformation at scale with periodic convenings and discussions of such efforts in light of the knowledge generated by applied research efforts is what we mean by Informed Dialogue. The publications prepared to support such dialogues are published using creative commons licenses in order to invite the rapid dissemination and adaptation of those ideas to various contexts, and to invite partnership in co-constructing and advancing a knowledge base that is reflective of practitioners' knowledge, often underrepresented in academic literature on the process of educational change.

Education systems have changed more than we think

Developed over two centuries ago as a byproduct of the Enlightenment, the institution of public education was an innovation designed to provide all people the opportunities to develop capabilities to improve themselves and the communities of which they are a part. Inherent to this institutional invention, therefore, is the aspiration of scale. The scale that public education has reached over the last century and a half is remarkable. Today, most children in the world go to school, a result of dramatic expansion in access which took place over the last century, especially significant given that it took place in a context of dramatic population growth. Almost two billion humans today are under the age of 25, and most of them spend a considerable period of their lives in educational institutions. Few products or services have scaled in the history of humanity the way in which basic education has in the last century. Since public education systems are typically the largest organizations in most societies, they represent also the best context in which to study and understand the challenges of producing change at scale.

Change at scale in public education has unfolded along two interrelated dimensions. The first: simply in the number of students that schools have included. The second: in the services delivered by schools to those students. Over the course of their history, educational institutions have expanded the definition of *who* should be educated—expanding the definition of what is meant by educating *all* children—as well as the definition of *what* competencies those children should gain in school, with the consequent expansion in the services necessary to help students gain these competencies.

I have elsewhere argued that the history of public education can be construed as the history of two competing social "projects." First, a conservative project that sees schools as conserving and preserving social structures and values; and, second, a progressive project that sees schools as capable of building a more inclusive social order (Reimers, 2006). Each of these competing projects has been defined by expectations about which students should be educated and by the purposes for which they should be educated. Institutional structures, norms, and practices have evolved to achieve those expectations

5

including, among others, curriculum standards, roles for educators, pedagogies, governance of schools, and approaches to assessment.

Examples of the expansion of the definition of who should be educated include the American civil rights movement and the global movement to educate students with special learning needs. The civil rights movement in the United States aimed to advance greater social inclusion and justice by expanding educational opportunities for African American children and other racial minority children who had been previously denied those opportunities, both in terms of access to school as well as real opportunities to learn. The global movement to educate students with special learning needs, the aspirations of which are reflected in the Salamanca statement and framework for action on special needs education, were adopted by the World Conference on Needs Education in Salamanca in 1994. These are examples of ongoing progressive efforts to expand the definition of "all" to truly include *all* children.

Further examples of the progressive project's efforts to expand the definition of *what*, exactly, should be learned in school include the stance adopted by Horace Mann by proposing that students should be taught to read by engaging with "big ideas" and authentic texts; the Progressive Education Movement in the United States advanced by John Dewey and his contemporaries; or the more recent global movement to promote the teaching of high order thinking skills, reflected for example in international assessments of student knowledge and skills such as the Organisation for Economic Co-operation and Development's (OECD) Programme for International Student Assessment (PISA).

The global movement to educate all children is therefore, by definition, an example of change at scale in the institutions of education. The opportunity to enroll in school and to learn what was intended in the curriculum has been "scaled" to include more and more children in ways that have outpaced the growth of the world's population. This has been done by identifying institutional structures, norms, and practices that enable such expansion and scaling them. Often this process has succeeded by recognizing practices which had been successful in some geographies, transferring them to different contexts, and then scaling them. Much of the assistance offered by international development education organizations such as UNESCO, UNICEF, or others to the global education movement has consisted of identifying such practices, transferring them, and supporting governments as they scale them. For example, much of the expansion in access to primary education during the 1950s was achieved by implementing practices such as "double shifts" of classes in the same school building, and in this way doubling the capacity of the existing infrastructure in order to enroll more children. Efforts to improve quality at scale have included the design and provision of textbooks and other instructional resources, the development of norms for teacher certification, and provision of teacher professional development in core academic subjects such as literacy, or mathematics, and the development of systems of assessment of student knowledge and skills.

The scaling of structures, norms, and practices to make education more "relevant" and more "empowering" of students has been more contentious, in part because of contestation over the specifics of which competencies actually empower children. There is, arguably, a developmental progression resulting from the contested nature of how to make education relevant. The divergent nature of views over what to teach and how make this truly an adaptive challenge. As consensus is reached over what to teach and how to do it, this becomes a technical challenge of improving quality. It is today easier to find consensus around the basic literacies of reading and writing, and perhaps numeracy, and therefore to scale practices aimed at supporting their development as has been done extensively in the past. This was not always the case, however, and veritable "wars" were fought over discussion of what it meant to learn to read, learn math, or learn science.

Today, consensus around whether other competencies are empowering, and should therefore be part of the mix of universal public education, is more elusive. For instance, in the year 2000, the OECD launched a program to assess higher order skills in the areas of literacy, mathematics and science, the Programme of International Student Assessment (PISA). These cross-national assessments were designed to evaluate the extent to which 15-year-olds who were enrolled in school had the necessary skills to participate in a knowledge based economy and in democratic societies. This assessment has generated valuable information about the levels of skills demonstrated by youth and the disparities in the skill levels among various groups within the countries participating in these studies. But, this information has not been received with the same enthusiasm everywhere. Education leaders in some nations have withdrawn from participating in these assessments; others have openly challenged the assessment as an interventionist attempt on the part of the OECD, controlled by nations that industrialized earlier, to impose a particular educational model. Even more elusive is consensus on the ways to help students develop as whole children, attending to their socio-emotional as well as cognitive development.

Elusive as the consensus may be over what makes education relevant and empowering, there is no question that the acceleration of changes in the social context of schools makes it imperative to keep searching for ways to make education matter to the lives students live and will live in the future. Even as the goals of education remain to prepare students to be self-authoring and to improve the communities of which they are a part, the specific skills and dispositions that should be gained in school need to evolve to keep up with changes in social organization and production. As artificial intelligence increasingly allows computers to do tasks that humans previously did, this changes the skill requirements for economic participation. As technology changes the ways in which people organize, relate to each other, or participate civically, new skills are necessary to do those things in ways that are mediated by technology. As the demographic composition of communities changes because of globalization, new dispositions are necessary to develop the trust and civility which are indispensable for humane and civil community participation and social interaction. To sum up, elusive as the consensus over what competencies will make education more relevant may be, it is essential that schools engage in the search for ways to become more relevant. The special challenge will be to engage in such a change process without complete knowledge to guide it, and to design a process of change in such a way that it can help generate some of that knowledge. It is because of the special nature of this challenge that bringing relevancy enhancing reforms to scale is not the same as scaling efficiency enhancing change.

In spite of these challenges, calls for such change efforts have been slowly developing over the last two decades. Beginning in the 1990s, a number of academics, government agencies, and international organizations argued that technological change, and the transformation of the economy it would bring about, would require rethinking of the competencies that students should gain in school in order to obtain employment and to add value to the economy (Murnane & Levy, 1996; Rychen & Salganek, 2003; Unesco, 1996). A concurrent set of ideas proposed that increased demands of civic participation would require more intentional efforts to help students gain the skills and dispositions that would enable political efficacy (Torney-Purta et al., 2001; Levinson, 2012; Levine, 2000). Other analysts argued that globalization would call for specific education for global competency (Boix Mansilla & Jackson, 2011; Zhao, 2010). In response to these developments, a wave of recent curriculum reforms around the world provide the policy context to provide students expanded educational opportunities to gain these competencies (Reimers & Chung, 2016).

Numerous educational innovations in educational structures, programs and practices have been developed to align with these expanded educational aspirations. Given the goals of public education to provide educational opportunities to all, and given the scale of the enterprise, it follows that a central preoccupation of public education leaders should be to understand how to scale effective programs that make education more relevant. While a fair amount is known about scaling educational change to improve access or quality, most of what is known does not draw on efforts to make education more relevant.

Three forms of educational change at scale

One form of educational change focuses on achieving goals over which there is consensus, for which solutions are relatively well known. As described above, these may include getting schools to serve more children, or to serve them better by teaching more effectively what most people agree should be learned in school (such as the basic literacies). These goals can be achieved by expanding the percentage of children enrolled in basic education, extending the duration of basic education, improving the effectiveness of programs to support initial literacy instruction, or increasing the effectiveness of schools in teaching students the intended curricular goals. In those cases, the goals are likely to be relatively uncontroversial, and there are likely optimal technical ways to achieve them on which there is sufficient consensus among key stakeholders to support change at scale. Even as there may be fewer challenges to persuading key stakeholders of their merits, the challenges to achieving such reforms at scale can still be significant. Fortunately, there is a body of knowledge about how to scale such efforts that can be drawn upon. Scaling such reforms requires identifying technical ways to do it—optimal school size and design, solutions such as the double shift schools, mapping the construction of new schools in the appropriate locations, and so on— obtaining the resources necessary to procure the essential inputs, and organizing and managing the tasks of converting those inputs into results such as new classrooms, new school buildings, more students enrolled, new programs to support literacy instruction, or programs of professional development to help teachers develop new skills. I will call this kind of scaling *scaling to enhance educational efficiency.*

An alternative form of educational change involves defining new goals—aligning the goals of schools with new trends and demands in society. An example would be deciding what role arts education, or sports, or entrepreneurship education should have in the curriculum; or determining how to foster active citizenship among students; or whether students should be educated to understand climate change. In those cases, the goals may be contested and there are no singular approaches to achieve them (much less consensus over how to do it). As a result, there are numerous challenges to deciding what to do and how. Scaling such reforms is initially largely about social dialogue among key stakeholders; subsequently, it is about collective learning, ongoing learning, and adaptation. Only once those processes have been addressed can the management of the tasks necessary to achieving such goals begin, and even then, the consensus that sustain possible progress may be elusive over long periods and necessitate continuous learning and negotiation. I will call these forms of change *scaling to seek educational relevancy.* As mentioned earlier, a relevancy enhancing reform may, over time, become efficiency enhancing once consensus is reached on the importance of the new goals and on how to reach them.

Fortunately, given that education systems serve about 2 billion people globally, there is an emerging knowledge base about how to scale efficiency seeking reforms on which we can build. As mentioned, the fact that more is known about this process does not mean it is easy. I will illustrate this knowledge base drawing briefly on five approaches to the study of large scale change, two of which have been specifically developed studying education change efforts.

A classic analysis of the formidable challenges involved in producing significant changes in instructional quality at scale is Richard Elmore's 1993 "Getting to Scale with Good Educational Practice." In this seminal essay, written two decades ago, Elmore argues that changing the core of instructional practice at scale is fraught with challenges because few change efforts address school organization and incentives, and those keep "the basic conventions of the core of schooling" (Elmore ,1996, p. 3) in place. Drawing on research on the Progressive Education Movement in the United States, and on large scale curriculum projects funded by the National Science Foundation in the 1950s and 1960s, Elmore shows that most of what changed in schools was peripheral, and not core to the way in which students and teachers engaged with content. From this analysis, he proposed four strategies to support the change of instructional practice at scale. The first: creating strong external normative structures for practice, such as performance standards for teachers, credentialing systems, or exemplars of good practice. The second: developing organizational structures that allow the teachers most committed to reform to influence their peers. The third: generating a robust theory about how to replicate success, which Elmore argues could emerge from experimentation based on existing theories of incremental growth, cumulative growth, discontinuous growth, unbalanced growth, or reproduction. Finally, the fourth strategy involved creating structures to promote learning of new practices and incentives to support them. (Elmore, 1996).

Aligned with Elmore's proposition that attention to structures is necessary to support changes in instructional practice is Sir Michael Barber's concept of "deliverology." While not developed specifically for the education sector, this approach posits that policy change necessitates an implementation strategy that relies on identifying the delivery chains that permit the translation of objectives into activities and eventually into results. These chains involve the creation of a delivery unit,the translation of the strategy into operational goals measured by a system of indicators to monitor implementation, and the establishment of routines to achieve behavioral change that will produce changes in the indicators (Barber, Moffit, & Kihn, 2011).

11

Along similar lines, the organization Management Systems International (MSI) has developed a framework to scale up large-scale change that highlights four elements: developing the vision; identifying the model; establishing the pre-conditions for scaling up; and monitoring, learning, and evaluation. Establishing the vision requires clarity regarding the unmet needs and the beneficiaries the scale up effort will address. Identifying the model involves an ex-ante analysis of the strengths and weaknesses of the model that will help achieve the vision, and identifying the requirements to persuade key-decision makers. The establishment of pre-conditions for scale requires securing necessary new resources and skills, necessary organizational changes, and mobilizing support. Finally, monitoring and learning involves assessing whether the scaling up process is on track and that information is used to maintain support (MSI, 2012).

The framework of change management developed by Jim Kotter and colleagues also offers very valuable insights into managing the scaling of efficiency-seeking reforms. As a result of studying how change efforts in business organizations succeed and fail, Kotter identifies the following stages in the process of managing change: establish a sense of urgency, form a powerful guiding coalition, create a vision, communicate the vision, empower others to act on the vision, plan for and create short term wins, consolidate improvements and produce more change, and, finally, institutionalize new approaches (Kotter, 2007).

One of the most complete and recent frameworks to study scaling up of quality education efforts has been developed by researchers at the Center of Universal Education at the Brookings Institute. The "Millions Learning" initiative has studied successful examples at scale of quality education focused on mastery of core academic content and higher order thinking skills. Their framework identifies the following four features of successful cases of quality at scale: committed leaders, delivery mechanisms, finance, and an enabling environment. Committed leaders who plan for scale from the outset by responding to local education needs, identify cost structures that are affordable at scale, clearly identifying core elements of the approaches while allowing adaptation of non-core features to local contexts, and mobilizing community expertise to support teachers. Delivery mechanisms include constructing educational alliances, mobilizing learning champions and leaders, deploying appropriate technologies, aligning with country priorities, and using data for institutional learning. Finance includes ensuring flexible education funding to support programs, stable and predictable long term financing, and financing to take pilots to scale. Finally, an enabling environment requires a supportive policy environment and a culture of research and development (Perlman-Robinson, Winthrop & McGivney 2016).

While knowledge about the process of scaling efficiency seeking educational change is helpful, there are unique aspects of scaling relevance enhancing reforms that deserve distinct theorizing. In the five approaches just mentioned, central to the process of bringing educational change to scale is obtaining support from the various stakeholders affected by such change. This support is proposed as being contingent on a clear understanding of what the change requires, on having the skills to advance it, and on seeing the expected change as aligned with the interests of each group of stakeholders. Understanding what change requires is easier in domains which have developed over a sufficiently long period that there is consensus on that success looks like, how to measure it, and how to produce it. Once such knowledge base exists, creating programs to help build the capacity to support that change becomes feasible. Negotiating the politics of efficiency seeking change is also easier, since the politics of such change--particularly those that involve expanding access typically expand resources—creating many opportunities for win-win situations. And, even when they require behavioral changes or adoption of new approaches to education, the demands they make and the risks they require are more limited.

Scaling educational reforms to make education relevant is not just a linear extension of scaling reforms to improve the efficiency of school systems—of their capacity to optimize in achieving established goals, over which there is consensus and where there are known technological solutions to such improvement. Scaling relevance-enhancing reforms requires creating the conditions for collaboration on provisional and fragile consensus on the purposes of education and on the translation of those purposes into institutional structures, norms, and practices in ways that are responsive to the unique demands of the national and local context, technological change, and individual characteristics of learners. Just as important, because relevance enhancing reforms act on a knowledge base that is emerging, advancing such reforms is especially about creating conditions where implementation is also an opportunity for learning.

As relevance enhancing reforms consolidate, and the learning it has allowed produces results, the process of scaling can become one of improving efficiency, because there is now consensus on the goals and the means to achieve them. Such transition from relevancy enhancing to efficiency enhancing usually takes place over long periods of time, when the ideas about what is relevance enhancing become so widely accepted that they become mainstreamed into the prevailing culture of education and part of the set of ideas about how to teach and what to teach. Expert knowledge, often produced by research, can normalize these new ideas into the established educational culture. For example, the "reading wars"—alternative conceptions over how best to foster the development of early literacy—eventually led to a consensus over the merits of a balanced approach to reading instruction, and such consensus was facilitated by expert synthesis of decades of scientific research on the subject, including a consensus report of the National Research Council. What were once new ideas about how to make reading instruction relevant, such as those advanced by Horace Mann, eventually became integrated into mainstream educational culture as a result of the development of a consensus on what outcomes were important, how to measure them, and of a body of scientific knowledge that illuminated the relative effects of alternative approaches to literacy instruction. This process took well over a century.

Thus, there are five key requirements to scaling relevance-enhancing reforms. Key in all of them is a learning orientation, an approach that allows continuous learning, refinement, and dissemination of the ideas that sustain instructional practice to help students gain competencies that are critical for an evolving future.

Creating conditions for…
     (1) … sustained provisional consensus on the purposes of education
          (2) … the translation of those purposes into institutional structures, norms, and practices

In ways which are responsive to...

     (3) ... the unique demands of national and local context,

     (4) ... technological change and other social trends

     (5) ... the individual characteristics of learners

Creating conditions for sustained provisional consensus on the purposes of education

Given the scale of the educational enterprise and the distributed nature of authority over the educational process, which involves parents, teachers, administrators, education policy makers, and a range of interest groups, consensus over what should be taught is difficult to achieve and always precarious, even more so consensus about what to teach in response to rapid changes and an uncertain future. Building and maintaining such consensus is essentially an exercise in communication, but not just of the kind proposed by Jim Kotter in his change management framework, or about Barber's "deliverology" approach, or the approach proposed by Management Systems International, which are about leadership communicating to subordinates the goals of change—typically in hierarchical organizations. Rather this is multi-way communication aimed at collective learning in individuals organized in networks of the kind discussed by Peter Senge in the book *The Fifth Discipline*, and in the applications of this work to the field of education (Senge, 2006).

Achieving such consensus requires mapping the networks—the groups with influence over the process—and orchestrating communications and negotiations among them in order to build a coalition that sustains support for the change efforts over an extended period(McGinn & Reimers, 1996). Creating this provisional consensus is essential to open the possibilities for educational innovations that are relevance enhancing. This requires building a new narrative about education, one that connects a vision about the achievement of desirable social goals, with the need for the development of new competencies in schools, and for a call to take the risk to experiment in taking on ambitious education goals. A powerful narrative is essential to cause people to change mindsets about what teaching and learning are, and to cause them to take some distance from existing norms and routines that lock so much instructional practice in place. For instance, the use of student assessments which typically focus on a narrow set of skills to support the improvement of education creates powerful incentives to align instruction to those domains which are measured. Many argue that the only way to change instruction is to change assessment, but expanding assessments to include new domains is, in itself, an adaptive challenge likely to face as much dissent as the notion that an expanded set of competencies needs to be taught. Hence there is a need for a narrative that makes the case for change and opens up opportunities for change, either through new curriculum frameworks, new assessment instruments, or new educational programs.

One of the issues that such provisional consensus on the need for ambitious goals for education must tackle is whether "21st century education" is a necessity or a luxury good. A prevailing mindset is that while competencies beyond the basic literacies are desirable, they can only be considered after the basic literacies have been attained, making such 21st century competencies a "nice to have," not a "need to have" commodity. In the contestation between conservative and progressive education projects I referenced earlier, it is generally the case that conservative groups fail to see as necessary for the children of subdominant groups the competencies that they consider essential for their own children, perhaps because they help maintain their privilege. At the core of the question of whether the global education movement to educate all children does in fact empower them is precisely the issue of what are the competencies which empower the poor.

Creating conditions for the translation of those purposes into institutional structures, norms, and practices

Ideas about purposes of education that are relevant need to be translated into specific observable outcomes or competencies that educators can understand and recognize, plans for how to assess student performance in those outcomes and provide feedback, and specific understandings of pedagogical practices that can help students develop those competencies. Instruments such as protocols, assessment rubrics, curriculum, and supplementary resources are essential to enabling large and diverse groups of educators distributed across many different institutions to engage in coherent practices that provide students consistent opportunities to gain such competencies. Because these tools and frameworks need to be generated based on emerging and evolving ideas about what competencies matter, the process of development of such instruments to support instructional change is less one of creating the "deliverology" that Barber and colleagues propose, and more similar to the application of Improvement Science to Education, as Tony Bryk and his colleagues describe in their book *Learning to Improve*.

One obstacle to advancing relevancy enhancing reforms is that the concept of '21st century education' is not just not considered a necessity, but that it is poorly understood, or fuzzy. Policy can, of course, provide an enabling context for relevancy enhancing reforms even if policy is not self-executing. Curriculum standards and student assessments have the virtue of making such concepts operational in ways which can be understood by the many education stakeholders whose concerted action is necessary to open space for relevancy enhancing reforms. This is no small task, as the resistance still faced by the PISA assessments of the basic literacies in some quarters illustrate.

The development of practices that are relevancy enhancing requires experimentation and learning from such experiments at multiple levels. Policy can create an enabling environment to support such experimentation, for example supporting the development of partnerships between organizations of civil society, such as universities, or think tanks, and schools as well as the creation of school networks. But learning requires more than a context with the freedom and the incentives to try new practices—it requires systematic collection of information about results and integrating it into a cycle of reflection and revision of innovative practices.

Responsive to the unique demands and opportunities of national and local context

Uniform standards and instruments that ensure consistency and coherence across sites need to be balanced with enough flexibility in schools and classrooms that allow teachers to respond to the unique characteristics and needs of their social contexts. This requires the development of high levels of teacher expertise—of professionalism. Scaling relevance enhancing reforms requires, then, high levels of investment in the development of teacher professionalism, not only in teaching teachers new content or techniques, but more generally in building their capacities to be highly expert in addressing the needs and opportunities created by the contexts in which they teach, as well as the particular needs and strengths of their individual students. Such development requires building work environments that are supportive of continuous learning and that activate the intrinsic motivation of teachers to continuously improve. This involves building the capacity of schools as organizations and of teams, rather than of teachers as individuals, and this calls for creating multiple learning opportunities in schools as organizations, so that learning all the time is part of the job.

Continuously responsive to technological change and other societal trends

The challenge of making education relevant in trying to respond to social and economic change is that the speed of this change is accelerating, creating a constantly moving target for the competencies that are relevant, other than the competency to adapt to change itself. This means scaling relevance enhancing reforms requires maintaining a balance between building a consensus on what the new institutions of education should be, while keeping such consensus open and continuously evolving to changing trends. Strategy in this context becomes continuous learning and adaptation. Paradoxically, this requires stability of teams of teachers and school leaders, and persistence in efforts of improvement, so that it is possible to actually learn from them, and to discern with intelligence what adaptations to make to changes in context.

Responsive to the individual characteristics of learners

Relevant education can only be relevant to individual students, helping each of them make sense of their strengths and ways of adapting to and responding to the circumstances of their lives. Just as teachers need to be able to balance the consistency of uniform aspirations and standards with the opportunities and needs of their school and social contexts, they also need to be able to personalize their instruction. This means recognizing their students as individuals, and providing them opportunities to build on their own interests and strengths, address their individual needs, and progress at their own pace. This requires high levels of expertise from teachers and, as such, scaling reforms to

18

make education relevant involves investing in the development of such professional expertise.

To conclude, when Jean Baptiste Alphonse Karr, a Parisian teacher and editor of Le Figaro, stated about change "plus la change plus c'est la meme chose" (Karr 1849) (the more things change, the more they remain the same) the modern French education system did not yet exist. The creation of public education, in France and elsewhere, shows that in fact things have changed quite a bit for humanity in a short period of time by creating institutions that have successfully integrated most of humanity in a common invented experience. That silent revolution, however, perhaps the most significant humanity has experienced, is not all of one cloth: it combines three different forms of change at scale. Understanding the nuances of such successful and failed attempts to change at scale who should be taught, what should be taught, and in what way, is critical to help us steer these wonderful institutions we have invented in the direction of empowering all students to live good lives and to improve the world.

Fernando M. Reimers is the Ford Foundation Professor of the Practice of International Education and Director of the Global Education Innovation Initiative and of the International Education Policy Masters Program at Harvard University. An expert in the field of Global Education, his research and teaching focus on understanding how to educate children and youth so they can thrive in the 21st century.

References

Barber, M., Moffit, A., & Kihn, P. (2011). *Deliverology 101: a field guide for educational leaders.* Thousand Oaks, CA: Corwin Press.

Bryk, A. S., Gomez, L. M., Grunow, A., & LeMahieu, P. G. (2015). *Learning to improve: how America's schools can get better at getting better.* Cambridge, MA: Harvard Education Press.

Elmore, R. (1996). Getting to scale with good educational practice. *Harvard Educational Review, (66)*1,1-27.

Glewwe, P. and K. Muralidharan (2015) Improving School Education Outcomes in Developing Countries: Evidence, Knowledge Gaps, and Policy Implications. Oxford. Center for Global Development. http://www.bsg.ox.ac.uk/sites/www.bsg.ox.ac.uk/files/documents/RISE_WP-001_Glewwe_Muralidharan.pdf

Heifetz, R. A., Kania, J. V., & Kramer, M. R. .(2004). Leading boldly — Foundations can move past traditional approaches to create social change through imaginative – and even controversial – leadership. *Stanford Social Innovation Review, (Winter 2004)*.

Karr, A. (1849) Les Guêpes. (Paris: Michele Levy Freres, Editeurs). https://archive.org/details/lesgupessrie00karrgoog

Kofter, J. P. (2007). Leading Change. Why Transformation Efforts Fail,". *Harvard Business Review, 92*, 107.

Levine, P. (2000). *The new Progressive Era: Toward a fair and deliberative democracy*. Lanham, MD: Rowman & Littlefield.

Levinson, M. (2012). *No citizen left behind*. Cambridge, MA: Harvard University Press.

MSI. (2012). Scaling up—From vision to large-scale change: A management framework for practitioners. Washington, DC: Management Systems International.

Mansilla, V. B., & Jackson, A. (2011). Educating for global competence: Preparing our youth to engage the world: Asia Society.

Murnane, R. J., & Levy, F. (1996). *Teaching the new basic skills: Principles for educating children to thrive in a changing economy*. New York: Free Press.

Reimers., F. M. (2006). Social progress in Latin America. In Bulmer-Thomas, V., & Coatsworth, J. (Eds.). *Cambridge Economic History of Latin*

America. Vol II. (pp. 427-480). Cambridge, UK: Cambridge University Press.

Reimers., F. M. (2015a). Educating the children of the poor: A paradoxical global movement. In Tierney, W. (Ed). *Rethinking Education and Poverty.* (pp. 18-37). Baltimore: Johns Hopkins University Press.

Reimers, F. M., & McGinn, N. (1997). *Informed dialogue: Changing education policies around the world.* Westport, CT: Praeger Publishers.

Reimers, F. M., & O'Donnell, E. B. (Eds.). (2016). *Fifteen letters on education in Singapore.* Raleigh, NC: Lulu Publishers.

Reimers, F. M., & Chung, C. K. (Eds.). (2016). *Teaching and learning for the twenty-first century.* Cambridge, MA: Harvard Education Press.

Perlman-Robinson, J., R. Winthrop, and E. McGivney. 2016. *Millions Learning: Scaling up Quality Education in Developing Countries.* Washington, D.C.: Brookings Institution

Rychen, D. S., & Salganek, L. H. (Eds.). (2003). *Key competencies for a successful life and a well-functioning society* Gottingen: Hogrefe and Huber.

Senge, P. M. (2006). *The fifth discipline: the art and practice of the learning organization.* New York: Doubleday/Currency.

Torney-Purta, J., Lehmann, R., Oswald, H., & Schulz, W. (2001). *Citizenship and education in twenty-eight countries: Civic knowledge and engagement at age fourteen.* IEA Secretariat, Herengracht 487, 1017 BT, Amsterdam, The Netherlands.

UNESCO. (1996). *Learning: The treasure within: Report to UNESCO of the International Commission on Education for the Twenty-first Century.* Paris: UNESCO Publications.

Zhao, Y. (2010). Preparing globally competent teachers: A new imperative for teacher education. *Journal of Teacher Education, 61*(5), 422-431.

Scaling 21ˢᵗ Century Education

Charlie MacCormack, Senior Fellow, Interaction. President Emeritus, Save the Children.

Introduction

The world is undergoing one of its greatest transitions—comparable in scope to the change from hunting and gathering to agriculture, and from agriculture to manufacturing and industrial production. As with those earlier transformations, the current transition from the Industrial Age to the Age of Technology and Science will bring dramatic changes to social, cultural, and political life, as well as to the systems of socialization and education through which children and young people are prepared to respond positively and productively to their external environment. It is not the purpose of this essay to describe the content and delivery of the appropriate forms of adaptive education, but much has been written that does this.

Allow me to begin with a plea to rebrand "Education for the 21ˢᵗ Century." First, it will become less and less meaningful as the century marches on. Best to change the framing now, before it gains wide currency. Secondly, it does nothing to describe the actual content of what we are trying to do. Instead, I propose something like "Education for an Age of Technology," or "Education for an Age of Change"— one of those would serve us better. (Yet, having said this, for purposes of convenience and consistency, I will use "Education for the 21ˢᵗ Century" throughout this essay.)

Why scale 21st century education?

21ˢᵗ century education is not a prize for those who successfully complete 20ᵗʰ century education, however modified by a few group and experiential activities. Rather, it entails a student possessing the values, knowledge, skills, and behaviors necessary for successful engagement with an age of technology, change, globalization, and cultural, political, and workplace turmoil. Elites around the world are already ensuring that their children receive this type of technological and multicultural education, and it would definitely further entrench the growing inequality currently dominating global economic change to deny the poorer majority access to an education appropriate for the current era.

At the Think Tank that brought us together at the Harvard Graduate School of Education symposium in October 2016, a thoughtful Latin American education leader suggested that, given scarce resources, it would be politically and perhaps ethically inappropriate to deny investment in basic schooling such as literacy and numeracy in order to advance 21st century education. Approaching investment in education as a zero sum decision between basic literacy and numeracy versus 21st century competencies would be a grave mistake. We need to design affordable country-appropriate lifelong education systems that deliver basic education *as well as* 21st century competencies. For many countries, this will require bypassing facilities-based schooling beyond the elementary years. Exactly fifty years ago James Coleman noted that "schools were created for a world that was experience rich and information poor. Now we have a world that is information rich and experience poor." Yet even after five decades we continue to replicate 20th and even 19th century models of schooling.

Throughout the world, today's students enter school and live their lives generating most of their learning through electronic media. Growing school drop-out rates in the later years in country after country demonstrate that today's young people are "voting with their feet" against traditional school-based education in the higher grades. This suggests that poor and middle income countries—which in any case have no fiscal possibility of replicating the capital- and labor-intensive educational models of Western Europe and North America—should invest in technology- and group-based teaching and learning. Whole sectors such as telecommunications, banking, and even health care have bypassed costly Western models. and we should be much more serious about exploring similar models for education.

What are the barriers to scaling 21st century education?

(1) Specialized facilities-based schools, traditionally-trained teachers, school administrators, and educational bureaucracies represent some of the world's largest and most consistently-replicated interest groups, matched only by military and health institutions. Hundreds of billions of dollars have been, and continue to be, invested in maintaining and expanding this model. Teacher training institutes train teachers in the

same ways they have for decades. Teachers' unions defend these practices and their certification programs. Construction and transportation companies count on schools as a significant segment of their business. Without a market mechanism, this is not a system that will easily be replaced.

(2) Beyond the global consensus about school buildings and consistently-trained teachers that stand in front of students, there is no agreement on the basic goals and priorities of formal education. Some believe the inculcation of obedience and discipline in children is the principal goal. Others feel that the creation of "good citizens"—be they democratic, socialist, or nationalist—should be primary. Still others feel that the dissemination of religious orthodoxy is the priority. And then there is the delivery of whatever skills are perceived to be critical to success in the job market. The point is that without agreement on the foundational goals of education, it is virtually impossible to get cross-national replication of the best practices of 21st century education.

(3) Even if we had agreement on the fundamental goals and outcomes of 21st century education, we lack data that demonstrates that the outcomes agreed to by most 21st century educators can produce the social and economic benefits that are promised. There is even less data to show which technologies, delivery systems, and pedagogies best deliver the outcomes recommended by 21st century educators. Thus, if the experts cannot agree, how is the average citizen to endorse a radical reformation in the content of their children's education?

What is to be done?

The road to scaling 21st century education at the global level will be neither straight nor smooth. Opposition from entrenched interests will be fierce. Organizing and strengthening advocates will be difficult since there are not a lot of benefits to taking on a large and entrenched system. Much of the potential success will likely come from innovations in the private sector and will not be easily transferred to large government bureaucracies. The beneficiaries—children and young people—have little political power and are more likely to opt out than to engage with a long-term change process.

Nonetheless, twenty-five years from now, 21st century education will be widely practiced. The countries and states/provinces that scale it will be better off economically and more stable politically. The private sector will demand it from their governments and will fund alternative models in the meantime. Social entrepreneurs will pioneer more and more options and alternatives. Young people will design more of their own technology-enabled learning. The tax costs of 21st century education might well be less than traditional school systems. Over time, governments will adopt an increasingly-accepted approach that involves decreasing political risk. But how might this process be rationalized and accelerated?

(1) Build a long-term cross-national research program that measures the economic, social, and personal outcomes of 21st century learning. Additionally, compare the cost-effectiveness of different delivery systems in different national settings. UNESCO or the World Bank are presumably the logical candidates for this task. It will need to be sustained for several decades, and the results will need to be widely disseminated. Without the evidence and a relative consensus from experts, scaling at the global level will be impossible.

(2) Identify governors and mayors in large multiethnic countries willing to model 21st century education in their jurisdictions. Focus particularly on teacher training reform in these locations, and encourage multilateral organizations and foundations to fund such initiatives. Building the private and multilateral donor base for models of 21st century education is an essential step in the coming decade, as a precursor to widespread adaptation at the governmental level.

(3) For example, the Harvard Graduate School of Education (HGSE) can elevate its convening role around scaling 21st century education by bringing together leading educational donors, such as the World Bank, UNESCO, the Gates Foundation, MasterCard, Hewlett, Packard, Banyan Tree, etc. The meeting should be structured around the most highly leveraged ways to accelerate 21st century education.

Secondly, convene a similar gathering of the large global organizations that are collectively implementing billions of dollars of educational programs in scores of countries. Among these global educational players are UNICEF, World Vision, Save the Children and Plan

26

International. They are in a position to model, evaluate and advocate for 21st century global education in a multitude of countries.

HGSE can also sponsor an annual award for the political or other leader who has done the most to expand 21st century education—a kind of Nobel Prize for 21st century educational leadership. The Hilton Humanitarian Award is an example of this in another sphere. The media finds this type of award an attractive story, and it would serve to incentivize decision-makers to take educational reform more seriously. Finally, there should be an annual publication, similar to UNDP's Human Development Report, that ranks the world's 200 countries on how well they are doing in transforming their educational systems to the demands and opportunities of an age of mass information technologies. Political leaders have shown an inclination to take these rankings seriously.

In conclusion

Information technologies have transformed the global economy and its workforces. They are rapidly destroying the hierarchical organizational models of the 19th and 20th centuries. People are communicating, learning, and socializing in entirely new ways. Human society is rapidly abandoning the types of interactions upon which schooling is still based. The world's wealthiest countries and global elites have already embraced participatory, experiential, technology-enhanced, multicultural education. If we are to avoid increasing the already unacceptable degree of inequality across and within countries, it is essential that we accelerate the adaptation of evidence-based, affordable 21st century education.

Charles MacCormack is currently an advanced Leadership Fellow at Harvard University, where he is working on issues involving the role of private philanthropy in global health and development. Most recently, Dr. MacCormack has served as Executive Chair of the Millennium Development Goal Health Alliance; Executive in Residence at Middlebury College; and Senior Fellow at Interaction. He was previously CEO of Save the Children from 1993 to 2012 and CEO of World Learning/School for International Training from 1997 until 1993. He is a graduate of Middlebury College and holds Masters and Ph.D degrees from Columbia University.

Redefining educational quality: a 21st century understanding of student achievement in Latin America

Luis E. Garcia de Brigard, former Deputy Minister of Education - Colombia

The advent of international student assessments a few decades ago led to the stark realization that pupils in Latin America were lagging behind their peers from most middle- and high-income countries. The region's students were consistently placed at the bottom of the rankings, and the issue of student performance became a regular topic in the media and an increasingly common matter during political campaigns. Albeit with some reluctance, more and more countries decided to participate in international assessments—most notably the OECD's PISA and UNESCO's Regional Comparative and Explanatory Studies. This process, along with the rise of civic organizations and a generalized sophistication of public educational leadership, has led to a renewed interest in education which has in turn yielded significant progress in student performance in most Latin American countries during recent years.

Unsurprisingly, the common understanding of the challenges ahead is mostly defined by what international student assessments have pointed to be the most salient shortfalls of the region's students: performance levels on math, language, and science. In fact, this has largely become the very definition of educational quality and has shaped the public agenda in unprecedented ways. Unfortunately, the long and tortuous journey to raise awareness around educational quality seems to have become outdated. While international literature continues to accumulate evidence around the importance of developing and supporting 21st century education, most Latin American countries have embarked on a race to improve performance, as measured and defined by traditional standards –basic literacy and numeracy-, that do not necessarily reflect the holistic and multidimensional approach that lies at the core of 21st century education.

I believe, however, that the region can successfully fine tune its course, and in the process make a leap that can exponentially accelerate its progress and close the performance gap that remains the biggest threat to Latin America's future. Instead of pursuing the incremental gains that the world's leading countries had to pioneer, Latin American nations have an unprecedented opportunity to fast track its progress by targeting 21st century education as their primary goal, rather than interpreting it as a luxury that can only be afforded once the basic building blocks of literacy and numeracy have been thoroughly laid.

A tale of luxury and necessity

The last quarter of the 20th century was characterized by a vigorous effort to address issues of access in Latin America. By 2000, the region had reached net enrolment rates of over 90% in primary and only slightly lower in secondary. As is now the case with quality education, the quest for access was largely triggered by the emergence of comparative data that highlighted the dramatic reality of schooling in the region. Millions of children were unschooled, few pupils completed high school, and infrastructure was precarious. Governments raced to implement measures that would allow them to reach every child, rich or poor, living in the cities or in rural areas. Most opted to implement double shifts to expand the existing capacity of schools. Some adopted innovative methodologies like Escuela Nueva, which trained and empowered teachers and students to effectively run multi-grade schools in rural areas. Several countries deployed conditional cash transfer programs to incentivize enrollment and discourage dropouts. All in all, the goal of higher enrollment was achieved, and most countries in the region were able to claim mid- pack or even lead places in the global race for access.

However, just as countries celebrated their success, the tradeoff became apparent: the early results of international assessments showed that the region had neglected to pursue education quality. In the face of scarce resources, quality seemed like a luxury. The prevalent idea was that access had to come first and quality would have to be a future concern. As a result, governments effectively left quality on the back burner. By the time the comparative assessments gained popularity, it seemed too late. The performance gap seemed insurmountable and for many Latin American countries it felt like it was back to square one.

The need for 21st century education in Latin America, I am afraid, is currently considered a luxury, just as quality education was a few decades ago. While pioneering countries across the globe are conscientiously revising their curriculums to reflect the needs of 21st

century learners, most Latin American countries are devotedly focused on improving test performance in math and language (and as the latest PISA results have showed, some of them are doing it successfully).

This view is understandable. To many, the benefits of 21st century education still sound too academic and its implementation seems far too challenging and expensive—much like quality sounded 20 years ago. However, the dangers of procrastination are all too apparent. The region cannot afford to defer the efforts to provide a 21st century education for every child. If Latin America fails to adapt, it may be too late and the gap may, yet again, prove to be insurmountable. Just as several countries—especially in Asia—have been able to simultaneously target access and quality with remarkable success, Latin America has the opportunity to embrace the challenge of 21st century education as a lever, rather than a tradeoff to quality.

Furthermore, the current economic challenges faced by Latin American countries make 21st century education even more urgent. A significant portion of the economic growth experienced during the last two decades (which has yielded enormous social progress in the region) was the result of a historic surge in the price of commodities. This, no doubt, allowed the region to reduce poverty and inequality, invest in education and other social programs, and consolidate stronger internal economies. The future, however, is more complicated. The international price of commodities is diminishing and Latin American economies have experienced very modest growth in recent years. Sustained growth will depend on the countries' ability to participate in a knowledge-based economy that rewards innovation, entrepreneurship, and sustainability. Equipping students with these skills must therefore be regarded as seriously as performing well in math, language, and science.

Tailwinds

While the topic of 21st century education is mostly foreign to the public and to policymakers in Latin America, there are a number of factors that may yield a favorable environment for implementing reforms in the right direction. First, the widespread implementation of extended school days by eliminating the double shift system has opened a healthy debate around what must be taught and learned during these longer school days. The experiences in Uruguay, Argentina, Colombia, Ecuador, Peru, and Chile, among others, have shown that most stakeholders favor the implementation of non-traditional academic programs, as well as sports and arts during the longer days in school. Examples at the regional and national levels indicate a decided effort to offer learning experiences that develop areas that have historically been sidelined by traditional education, such as project based learning, English as a second language, entrepreneurship and experiential learning. Most of these experiences, however, are still far from qualifying as rigorous 21st century education. There is a clear need for robust curriculum and training that will equip schools to offer high-quality programs. Notwithstanding this obvious challenge, the extension of the school day in most Latin American countries offers a unique opportunity to advance efforts geared towards the adoption of 21st century curricula.

On a different front, an equally powerful opportunity arises from the revamping of international assessments, particularly PISA. The adoption of measures that target critical thinking and the use of digital tools, for example, signal to participating countries the need to upgrade their curricula to equip their learners to face much broader challenges than those that can be tackled through rote memorization. While a few governments in Latin America still refuse to participate in comparative studies, the impact of these assessments in shaping policy in the region is undeniable. Governments are being held accountable for the performance of their countries in these exercises, and this provides reason to believe that ministries of education will respond to upgrades in international assessments by overhauling their own measures of learning, curricula, and professional development practices. Some countries have even implemented non-academic measures to their national assessments. Colombia, for example includes measurements of civic competencies in its standardized tests.

Other interesting examples that may accelerate the scale of 21st century education come from non-traditional actors like the International Baccalaureate (IB). While traditionally focused on elite international schools, the IB has extended its reach to a much wider audience of schools, and at the same time has focused its pedagogical efforts on developing a learner profile consistent with the demands of the 21st century. Interestingly, Ecuador has become a pioneer country in adopting the IB for public schools across its territory. This is an ambitious initiative that other countries are already following, and one that promises a departure from traditional approaches to teaching and learning.

After you

Critics often minimize the role of international actors in the shaping of educational policies. The reality is that the impact of these organizations on the destiny of Latin American educational systems has been notable. From the efforts of the Inter-American Development Bank (IADB) and the World Bank in promoting and financing school access and quality, to the influence of UNESCO and the OECD in measuring learning and suggesting pathways to achievement, the region has largely benefited from the implementation of proven initiatives. Generally speaking, whenever public leadership has been open to methodically adopting and adapting robust programs and technologies that have been piloted abroad, it has achieved progress and success, resulting in dramatic improvements for children. While this does not mean that Latin American countries are unable to pioneer initiatives—several innovations prove this point—it is undeniable that the current efforts to promote 21st century education are largely being promoted abroad. While some could see this as a disadvantage, the progress achieved in other geographies can be used as a unique opportunity to draft behind current advancements, thus building capacity without being left behind.

Furthermore, the circumstances under which Latin American governments embarked in a quest for access are dramatically different from today's circumstance. Four decades ago, many countries in the region were still low-income economies dependent on international aid to finance social programs. Democracies were still fragile, and in some cases nonexistent. Internal conflict was common, and education was at the bottom of national agendas. Moreover, there was still no international consensus or clearly defined collective goals around education, and the knowledge base was much more limited and dramatically less accessible. The marked growth of the region's economies, the consolidation of democracy in most countries, the increasing relevance of education in national policies, and the globalization of the education agenda since that time represent a stark contrast. Instead of the helplessness of the past, today Latin American countries are experiencing unprecedented levels of empowerment that allow them to better apply and ultimately contribute to the advancements being made in terms of 21st century education.

As such, countries that choose to commit themselves to promoting 21st century learning in their school systems will have a clear head start and a much gentler ride than they did when facing the challenges of access or quality. It will be up to political leaders and advocacy organizations to seize this unparalleled opportunity to fast track progress and achievement for all children.

Teamwork

The past few decades have demonstrated that a coordinated effort by different stakeholders can promote successful transformations of educational policy in Latin American countries. As argued above, most of the progress achieved in terms of access and quality has been the result of the sustained efforts of a wide range of public, private and international organizations. In facing the challenge of scaling 21st century education it will be crucial to promote the participation of all these actors.

National and regional governments

During the last few decades, there has been a remarkable progress in the capacity of the educational leadership in Latin America. Senior officials, especially at the national levels, tend to have a clear understanding about the challenges of their countries and about the policy changes needed to face them. This explains the widespread consensus about issues like the importance of the teaching profession, the need for national assessments, and the relevance of curriculum and materials. However, the awareness around 21st century education is still very precarious. This highlights the urgency to update the knowledge base and capacity of local and regional governments in order to enable the implementation of policies directed to promote 21st century education

International organizations

The World Bank, the IADB and the OECD, among others, have historically had a very significant influence in shaping educational policy in the region. Generally regarded as legitimate sources of knowledge, these organizations enjoy a privileged position in influencing the future of education in Latin America. It is critical that they participate more actively in the debate around 21st century education by funding research and financing programs, drafting reports, and driving the conversation.

International student assessment organizations

By continuing to upgrade their tests to assess 21st century skills and competencies, the organizations involved in administering these exams will effectively promote policy changes within countries. The current consensus in the region around the importance of language, math, and science has been facilitated by the existence of these comparative studies. As such, it is reasonable to expect that as testes evolve, so will the understanding of educational quality in Latin America.

Private sector

The private sector has rapidly gained a prominent spot in shaping the destiny of education in Latin America. By increasing their involvement in philanthropic initiatives and advocacy groups, deploying innovative programs that are later scaled by the public sector, and facilitating the transfer of knowledge from other geographies, private stakeholders are now a key player in the education ecosystem. Not surprisingly, it is in the private sector where the region has seen the biggest advancements in promoting 21st century education. In fact, the vast majority of ongoing initiatives that exemplify the future of education are being championed by the private sector (some of which are showcased in this publication). If the region is going to succeed in embracing 21st century education before it is too late, the private sector has to lead the charge by piloting programs, strengthening its advocacy efforts, and transferring knowledge.

Final thoughts

The 21st century is an era of acceleration, efficiency, and amplification: information travels at light speed and without boundaries, innovation and knowledge determines winners and losers, economies react in real time, and human talent flows across the globe to locate the best rewards to its value-creation potential. These are precisely the reasons why Latin American countries should decisively incorporate 21st century learning across their classrooms. Interestingly, these are also the very reasons why this transformation can happen rapidly, cost effectively, and at scale. It is by seizing the endless tools and opportunities afforded by the fascinating era that we are living in that the region can upgrade its educational systems in the hopes of a better future for its people.

Luis E. García de Brigard *is the Chief Executive Officer of Educas Americas, an international investment firm that specializes in K-12 education. He previously served as Deputy Minister of Education of Colombia where he led efforts to reform the teaching profession, create effective measures of learning and promote school accountability.*

21ˢᵗ leaders needed!

María Carolina Meza, Business Leaders for Education Foundation, Colombia, Representative of REDUCA (Latin-American Network of Civil Society Organizations for Education)

The increasingly globalized world gives us the opportunity to easily access innovation from around the globe. At the Global Education Innovation Initiative (GEII) Think Tank we could feel that innovation in education is already happening all around. The reflections at the meeting where based upon a wide range of educational systems, and showed that we are a strong force that can push forward educational systems and make them prepared for the demands of the 21ˢᵗ century.

A good leader can make a group move from one way of thinking to another, eliciting the group´s capacity for change. Ronald Heifetz (1998) has described how, in this process, leaders are those able to identify the differences between adaptive and technical challenges, and to act accordingly. In essence, technical challenges are those where the answer is based upon specific technical knowledge that may or may not be currently available. If the solution exists, good leaders take it and applies it; if not, the solution resides in the investment of resources for developing new knowledge or technology to solve the problem. But, good leaders are especially needed when the answer to the challenge needs more than just a technical innovation—that is, when the challenges are adaptive. Putting it simply, an adaptive challenge demands a change of culture, of the social representations of the group, when the loyalties and the beliefs that guide common behavior need to change. Good leaders are precisely those who find ways to navigate adaptive challenges and to guide groups towards new frontiers.

This specification is not a minor one. If we want to tackle the enormous challenge of shifting the world´s educational systems to new, revitalized ones, that can give all kids and youth competencies for living in this new century, we need to ask ourselves, as educational leaders, if we are talking about an adaptive or a technical challenge. In this brief document, I want to reflect on this question, which I found fundamental in the conversations with the members of the GEII Think Tank's. I will argue that the answer mixes both types of challenges, the

37

adaptive being the most urgent and difficult. In the end, I will share some ideas around the incentives we need to build, and the type of leaders we need to be to tackle these challenges.

The pending technical challenges

The assumption behind the question of scaling is that there is a successful experience already in place that can bring benefits broadly. The GEII has made great efforts to show us that there is not only one, but are a wide range of models already in place that can be used as examples for shifting an educational system. This is a great news, in a technical sense! We have already developed good *vaccines* for one of the main problems of education, which have been successfully evaluated, and have shown proven results. These experiences have some commonalities that we can dissect for expanding them. Here are some of them:

The experiences show the need to first agree upon the *common goals* to be achieved. The experiences identified by the GEII have taken into account the close relationship between developing cognitive, interpersonal, and intrapersonal competencies, and have make it explicitly the objective of developing all of them as equally important priorities. Therefore, a pending technical challenge is to develop ambitious goals that include, as a priority, the development of not only cognitive skills, but also competencies such as critical thinking, creativity, and cooperation.

All of the experiences show different and diverse ways of teaching. Or, even better, they show a *focus on learning* rather than in teaching. There already exists a lot of literature about the benefits of active learning approaches. Not only, I insist, for acquiring cognitive skills, but also for the development of competencies for citizenship—such as citizens who actively participate in building a better world, for themselves and others. Expanding successful interventions and policies means changing most of the interactions in the classroom and making changes in learning environments. This means focusing more on developing challenging learning experiences than in defining long content-mastery goals for each class. The goal, therefore, is to fundamentally shift the way most classrooms in the world look. We need to see classrooms where kids are solving problems, where they are working with others

38

toward developing interesting projects together, where kids and youth are engaged passionately with learning.

The models we have seen also show that *evaluation matters*. Those efforts that are successful are not afraid of evaluation. On the contrary, they are clear about the ways to measure their impact, although many of them must deal with the challenge of a lack of rigorous methods for measuring 21st century skills in a standardized way. To develop a radical shift in the field of education, we need to develop better ways for measuring progress in those competencies. Some of the examples we have seen already show new ways of measuring key skills which is an important step in this direction.

There are also technical challenges related with designing new ways of *delivering*—in a massive, scaled way—all of these technical discoveries. The research done by the Brookings Institute (Perlman Robinson, Winthrop, & McGivney, 2016) on scaling education programs shows how programs that have been successful in scaling up were designed with up front thinking on a massive delivery (in terms of, for example, costs, flexibility, problem solving, and integration in the system). The technical challenge, then, is to design ways of making these innovations accessible and possible for any school.

A new world demands a new mentality

If the basic technical solutions are already invented, why is it that the system remains so obsolete? For me, the answer to this question has to do with culture. When we examine in depth the most successful educational systems of the world—in terms of preparing kids for the 21st century—we may notice plenty of legal, financial, and technical reforms, but at the heart of those that are successful are radical shifts in the way education is conceived. This is the most important and difficult challenge—changing the mentality throughout society about crucial questions including: What is learning? How do we learn? Why do we learn? Who should teach? How should the actors in the educational relate? …among other important questions. Shifting a culture, or many cultures, is a huge and complex task. Here are some ideas for starting such an enterprise:

Culture defines the way we see ourselves, others, and the world. In this sense, we need to work with *all actors in the system*—this will help us to see education in a different light. Changing mindsets does not necessarily happen with research evidence nor as a result of moral exhortation. The most effective way to change the culture is to create experiences that make people feel about and relate in a different way to things that matter to them. In this sense, we need all actors in the educational system to feel and experience what a 21st century education can be. We all grew up in traditional educational settings, and in a way we all feel that they worked fine for us. As a result, it is difficult for people to be disloyal to this learning paradigm, and to shift the way they teach/learn/approach education to a brand new one, particularly if they have never felt firsthand how a change in approach feels and the benefits that it can bring.

To change mindsets means to combat common beliefs and ways of seeing things that are taken for granted. So, a major task is to identify these shared beliefs. A common one is that a big shift in education is not needed. Or, that there are more urgent needs (for example making all kids have access to a school, to more hours of school, to more years of schooling, or making kids learn mathematics and literacy, etc.). This lack of *sense of urgency* makes 21st century competencies the last priority for many governments and actors in the system. Creating a sense of urgency among all actors must be a priority.

Another common false belief is that it is not possible to change the system. Many say that "the system is too complex to be radically changed." This lack of a *sense of possibility* discourages any efforts to make change, and make those trying to foster change look like strange and utopian radicals. We need to convince the world that it is possible to make radical changes, and to demonstrate how in our lives we have already seen radical changes happen. This goes hand in hand with a sense of learned helplessness in the system, where critical leaders, in positions of power, feel that it requires to much effort to make radical changes in the schooling system, and therefore quickly just give up.

There are also deeply rooted *ways of understanding teaching, learning, and leading* that must change to make schools places where 21st century competences can be developed. The traditional ways of understanding teaching encompass discipline and order as a value. For many educators, cooperative learning, debate, or problem-based learning mean too much chaos, too much noise, lack of discipline, and challenges to authority. But for developing creativity, cooperation, communication skills, and all sorts of socioemotional skills, some chaos is needed. We need a system that can embrace change, conflict, and dialogue—a system more like a democracy than a tyranny. We need a system that is comfortable not being so linear in the way it sees learning and development. Only then can our education systems make space for creativity and be open to a diversity of ways of learning. This means changing values and loyalties—typical adaptive challenges.

Of incentives and change

A major discussion during the Think Tank was around the incentives we need for change to happen. Why do we have to reinvent the wheel if it has functioned well thus far? Education, it is said, is the most successful social invention and the most widely disseminated; Why is it, then, that we need to change it? To think about the incentives that we need for this question to be successfully answered by all actors is crucial.

There need to be clear pressures from society, from the market, from the academy, and from each actor. We need to create both *external and intrinsic incentives*. Changes in the system must come from top down as well as bottom up, and must be facilitated by a middle layer that is thoroughly convinced of the need for a renewed system. Evaluation can help, by showing the correlation between hard and soft skills development. Also, research that shows, for example, the economic impact of developing 21st century skills through increases in labor productivity, democracy, peace, and other aspects of life in a society. But, as I said before, the most crucial incentive is the intrinsic one— that will come when everyone is made to feel that a change is possible, urgent, and needed.

21st century leaders for fostering 21st competences

In this short reflection, I wanted to show that the challenge of scaling up 21st century learning is both a technical and an adaptive one. In this sense, it demands committed leaders. But what kind of leaders? Some with precisely the kind of competences we want to foster in the system!

41

We need leaders who not only believe in 21st century competences, but leaders who can be a living example of them since they need to foster them in each actor of the education system. Let me describe roughly what this means:

(1) Educational leaders need to learn how to *communicate* better—and this means not only to transmit a message clearly, but to listen, to generate deep dialogue, and to create synthesis that encompasses different ideas.

(2) We must commit all our *critical thinking* abilities to the cause. The education system needs no more victimization. There are too many conversations where each sector blames the other for not doing the right thing. We must start being critical about our own role, to understand better the cultural barriers to change, and how to contribute to challenging those barriers in each of the places we work.

(3) We need to be much more *creative* in our approaches to this challenge. There is no need to reinvent what is already invented—meaning no need to reinvent all the technical devices that are already out there. Instead, we need to put our creativity to work to dismantle all the culture barriers that inhibit the movement toward 21st century competences.

(4) Finally, we need to become educational leaders that can *cooperate*. There are vast numbers of researchers, organizations, technocrats, NGOs, private organizations, etc. that are already developing 21st century educational experiences, but most are isolated projects that feel like lonely islands of innovation, or that feel like they need to compete with others to succeed. We need to understand that together we are stronger, and that only by developing a united community of practitioners we are going to make change happen.

María Carolina Meza is the CEO of the Businessmen for Education Foundation, in Colombia, and a representative of REDUCA (Latin-American Network of Civil Society Organizations for Education). She is a Psychologist and Philosopher, and she has worked as a consultant, researcher and practitioner, in education and social projects at the public, social and academic sectors. Her area of expertise has been peace and human rights education, so as teacher training.

References

Heifetz, R. (1998). *Leadership Without Easy Answers*. Cambridge, MA: Harvard University Press.

Perlman Robinson, J., Winthrop, R., & McGivney, E. (2016). *Millions Learning: Scaling up Quality Education in Developing Countries*. Washington, DC: The Brookings Institution.

Vision and Leadership: Key levers to scale 21st century education globally

Ken Kay, CEO, EdLeader21

From the moment Fernando Reimers invited me to attend the Global Think Tank at Harvard, I was looking forward to a tremendous opportunity to learn. I have been focused on 21st century education for the last 15 years—first, as the founding President of the Partnership for 21st Century Skills[1]; now, as the CEO of EdLeader21[2]—and the majority of my efforts have been devoted to work in the United States. But, here was an opportunity to consider perspectives from nine countries around the world; I intuitively knew there would be much to be gained from such a dialogue. I was also intrigued and challenged by the focus of the discussion: the "scaling" of 21st century skills.

While discrete examples of schools and organizations advancing 21st century education are familiar in many countries, our focus in these sessions was to address an increasingly common question: How might we advance a wider-scale, systemic adoption of 21st century education? This is a daunting challenge and a crucial focus for further dialogue and action.

I have organized this letter into two sections. In the first, I share some general reflections on our discussions of this question. In the second, I offer some recommendations to enhance collaboration across national boundaries in pursuit of this challenge.

General Reflections

I was struck by the power and pervasiveness of messaging about 21st century education in each of the countries that was represented. All of the participants seemed to agree that how this work is represented in its broadest context—how 21st century education is framed in public discourse—was critical to its potential implementation in schools.

---

[1] http://www.p21.org/
[2] http://edleader21.com/

An interesting discussion developed about whether there should be an agreed-upon, consistent, international definition of 21st century competencies. While some argued that globally standardized principles and outcomes would be helpful, my own belief is that each country should identify 21st century competencies tailored to their specific contexts. My perspective emerges from my last five years of experience working with school districts in the United States. Individual districts need to be able to customize their "profile of a 21st century graduate" to be responsive to the specific social, cultural, and economic imperatives of their communities. I think this is true at a broader scale as well.

Tailoring 21st century competencies to suit a country's context will depend on its leaders' capacity to cultivate national consensus. In our discussions at Harvard, it seemed that a few countries—most notably China and Singapore—are better situated than others to foster that kind of consensus. This will inevitably enable broader and faster scaling of their models at a national level. In other countries such as the United States—where national consensus is more difficult to catalyze for a variety of cultural and political reasons—scaling will ultimately depend on visionary school districts who are leading a grassroots and "bottom up" adoption of 21st century education.

I agree with one of our participants who worried that the prevailing definition of 21st century education in international discussions—such as this forum exploring global scaling—is too biased to the American context. While there are some wonderful examples of 21st century education in the United States, the lack of political will to implement a coherent 21st century education policy at the state and federal level undermines claims that the United States should dominate the global 21st century education dialogue. Other countries are moving substantially ahead in expanding their model at scale. These countries should become the international leaders of the global conversation.

Potential Areas to Enhance Global Collaboration

Vision

Participants in the Global Think Tank agreed that developing a clear, coherent, and explicit vision of 21st century education is a crucial driver of local implementation. At EdLeader21, our professional learning community for school and district leaders in the United States, member districts have been developing profiles of the 21st century graduate[3]. Districts share those profiles with one another—not with the intention of adopting a common profile, but in order to learn from the multiple perspectives provided by each other's visions. www.profileofagraduate.org

Similarly, I would suggest that future global dialogues on 21st century education would be enhanced by participants collecting and sharing their profiles of 21st century graduates, teachers, and leaders. Having a broad understanding of the underpinnings of various national efforts would help to focus continued dialogue by providing context to national implementation strategies and lending substance to our discussion of their impacts. This would support global collaboration by helping us determine which competencies countries share and, thus, the areas in which focused international cooperation could be fruitful.

Leadership

We agreed in our discussions how vital the challenge of "leadership training" has become to the goal of scaling 21st century education. I was impressed by exemplary leadership training models from Singapore and Mexico. In the United States, EdLeader21 superintendents are focused seriously on the challenge of developing the leadership capacity to expand and to enrich their districts' 21st century education efforts. To support their work, EdLeader21 is launching a new "Leadership Academy" to give teams from schools and districts the opportunity to develop their leadership skills by collaborating to address a specific 21st century challenge that they face. Our members recognize that their 21st century competencies need to be modeled by our schools' leaders and embedded in their professional cultures.

---

[3] See www.profileofagraduate.org for examples.

Future international dialogue would benefit from participants sharing about their national leadership development efforts.

Assessment
A general consensus emerged that assessment practice and policy are perhaps the most important levers for scaling 21st century education. This is the area where countries stand to gain the most from sharing their examples and collaborating on their refinement. Regardless of variations from one nation's vision of crucial 21st century competencies to another, assessment practice needs to shift across the board— from a focus on content mastery and memorization to a commitment to measure those competencies that matter most.

In EdLeader21, member school districts have collaborated to develop rubrics for 21st century competencies (creativity, collaboration, communication, and critical thinking/problem solving). They have implemented common performance tasks and shared their results with each other. Various countries could benefit from promoting similar collaborations tailored to common assessment goals. Such collaborations could help move the assessment of 21st century competencies forward for every school, district, and national system, and would provide a major boost to scaling efforts.

Research and Development
In their writings, Fernando Reimers and Connie Chung have noted that international research and development in 21st education has been profoundly inadequate, compared to research in other areas of social and economic transformation. Educational research and development has not been focused or funded effectively to advance a 21st century model of education. It has been primarily focused on the impacts of an antiquated model that is in dire need of transformation.

This should be a focus of continued dialogue between countries. International collaboration on educational research and development, with a focus on 21st century competencies, would develop a more substantial research base and lead to new breakthroughs on the best ways to teach and assess in the 21st century. Investment in such collaborations would yield significant and substantial returns for national and international scaling efforts.

Teacher Preparation

I was impressed by the ardor among participants calling for substantial changes in teacher preparation programs around the world. Many in the United States have nearly given up hope for dramatic changes in colleges of education: programs are currently way behind the times, seemingly intractable in their capacity to change, and prisoners to the antiquated state certification policies they are obligated to serve. I was impressed by the intensity of participants' professed commitments to take on this challenge.

Some participants suggested that we put pressure on teacher preparation programs globally by evaluating their commitments to 21st century pedagogy and assessment in their practices. The results of these evaluations could then be publicized to a global audience. I believe this focus is warranted and I hope we monitor global efforts to dramatically improve 21st century teacher preparation. Today, most colleges of education do not prepare teachers well for our current challenges. But we need teachers and leaders who will be ready not only to support systemic transformation, but also to lead more schools and districts through it.

Conclusion

Not only did I enjoy our global dialogue; I was thoroughly energized by it. I was surprised and intrigued to discover that, in some respects, 21st century education has been more substantially developed in other countries than it has in the United States. This means to me that those of us committed to 21st century education in the United States stand to gain a great deal just by listening to our global colleagues. Continuing global dialogue—anchored by enhanced sharing of approaches to national visions of 21st century competencies, leadership development, assessment practice, research and development, and teacher preparation—will, I hope, help all of us to ensure that every child is prepared by our schools to be successful in the 21st century.

Ken Kay *is the CEO of EdLeader21, a professional learning community of leaders committed to 21st Century Education. He was the founding President of the Partnership for 21st Century Skills and is the co-author of "The Leader's Guide to 21st Century Education: 7 Steps for Schools and Districts."*

Scaling Impact: A Focus on Flexible Adaptation, not Replication

Eileen McGivney, Research Associate, Center for Universal Education at the Brookings Institution

The term "scaling up" means many things to many different people. Too often it is assumed to be synonymous with simply growing, getting bigger, reaching more people. By this definition, schooling is a tremendous scaling up success story, spreading around the world, reaching ninety percent of the world's children in a relatively short time frame.

But scaling up is not just about getting bigger and reaching more people; we also need to ask, to what end? What is the impact that we want to achieve by growing a program? In many cases, doing more of the same for more people doesn't achieve that impact, and instead we need to think of different pathways to scale. This was the focus of Millions Learning, a project of the Center for Universal Education at the Brookings Institution, in which we aimed to understand how we can scale up impact in education, achieving the vision of every child accessing a high-quality education and attaining skills and competencies they will need to be successful.

I was fortunate enough to spend a day hearing about scaling successes and challenges from an impressive group of practitioners, policymakers and researchers at the Harvard Global Education Innovation Initiative (GEII) Think Tank. The room was certainly filled with hope that we already have many of the tools we need to provide a holistic education to every child in the world, thereby accomplishing the ultimate impact: a world in which all young people achieve literacy, numeracy, and are creative problem solvers, strong communicators, and effective collaborators. Most everyone in the room had a project, program, or school that was already moving this vision forward.

And yet it was clear to me that this was not a workshop on how to scale their project to more students or teachers. The topics we grappled with at the Think Tank were much more complex, focused on how we can accelerate a fundamental shift in education in which the entire ecosystem works to foster a breadth of skills that includes those outside traditional academic subjects. We discussed the importance (or unimportance) of terminology, data, and assessment; how to achieve equity in education; and how to build entirely new structures that will better respond to the needs of today and the future.

It struck me when Claudia Costin and Rafael Parente presented about their work in Rio de Janeiro building GENTE (Ginásio Experimental de Novas Tecnologias Educacionais), an experimental school for marginalized children. They asked themselves: What if we change everything? What if we start from scratch?

What they built is quite different from many schools in the world today, with classrooms and interior design modeled to encourage collaboration, and a curriculum that favored hands-on projects led by students. They offered a variety of learning opportunities, including lecture-style instruction on Fridays among the collaborative projects. In the end, this school of the future cost about 20 percent more than the regular government schools, but it also improved the students' academic and life skills.

The most interesting lesson though, was how Rafael and Claudia spoke about scaling its impact. They did not build another experimental school to look exactly the same, and then another and another until they had reached as many students as possible. Instead, the school has served as a way to encourage change throughout the system. Elements of the experimental school have been adopted by other schools in Rio, and peer-to-peer teacher training has helped spread some of the best practices. The important message, they emphasized, was showing that the government encouraged innovation.

I think this is a powerful example of how scaling 21st century learning to reach more children will require flexible adaptation across schools and contexts. Scaling up in these terms cannot be about perfecting one model and getting more and more students into it. When that is the focus, too often programs lose their effectiveness as they are further removed from additional resources, inspiring leadership, and valuable relationships.

In Millions Learning, we found that flexible adaptation was a key ingredient in the recipe for scale. The cases we studied exemplified the balance between replicating the core factors that are effective and allowing other elements to be adapted to each context. Rather than attempting to scale a model exactly as it was piloted, successful cases identified the "non-negotiables" that were required for their programs to improve learning. In the scaling literature this has been referred to as "what's fixed and what's flexible," and scaling up the "core content."

Sistema de Aprendizaje Tutorial (SAT) is a program in Latin America that uses a progressive student-centered curriculum in which tutors work with students and learn alongside them. While the curriculum and pedagogy are core to the program, most other elements are localized including how, when, and where students and tutors want to meet and study. In another case, Teach for All's more than 40 partner organizations commit to the mission and principles of the organization, but are free to adapt and implement the program as they see fit for the needs of their country.

This principle of scaling is particularly important for 21st century and holistic education. We know that competencies such as creativity, collaboration, and problem-solving cannot be added to curriculum, taught, and assessed the same way traditional academic subjects are. Instead, the approach of every school, district, and country may look very different while accomplishing a broader vision for education. For that reason, Claudia and Rafael's work in Rio is an inspiring new way to think of scaling ideas.

The GEII Think Tank workshop exemplified these principles as well, often bringing up the need to show stories and examples of what works to help inspire and give the tools to school leaders and others to make a change—not to look at scaling as the practice of making one program bigger. I think the work of all the GEII participants helps reinforce the idea that we need to help foster a culture of experimentation, or a culture of R&D—research and development—in education systems, so that more school leaders, teachers, and policymakers can adapt what we know about 21st century learning to their own contexts. To Claudia's point, governments can send a powerful message to schools when they actively encourage innovation. Along with schools and programs, they can also help encourage a shift in the way we think about scaling to one where we focus on adapting and spreading principles of what works.

53

The widely known education researcher John Hattie put it extremely well when lamenting that "one of our major limitations in education is that we have little interest in scaling up successful ideas, preferring to argue that 'my class is unique.'" It is true of course that context matters, but so does widening the impact of what works, allowing for adaptation in various contexts. From the GEII Think Tank, I felt that this valuable group was on the right track, helping to spread ideas and approaches with the faith that we can indeed provide high-quality, holistic education everywhere in the world.

Eileen McGivney is a Research Associate at the Center for Universal Education at the Brookings Institution, where her work focuses on accelerating progress in education for the world's most marginalized children, particularly looking to innovation, technology, and new models that hold promise for improving learning at scale.

References:

Perlman-Robinson, J., R. Winthrop, and E. McGivney. 2016. *Millions Learning: Scaling up Quality Education in Developing Countries.* Washington, D.C.: Brookings Institution

"GENTE - Ginásio Experimental de Novas Tecnologias Educacionais." Resources: Videos. Global Education Innovation Initiative. Accessed April 18, 2017. https://globaled.gse.harvard.edu/videos

Kwauk, C. and J. Perlman-Robinson. 2016. *Sistema de Aprendizaje Tutorial: Redefining rural secondary education in Latin America.* Millions Learning Case Study. Washington, D.C.: Brookings Institution

John Hattie, "What Works Best in Education: The Politics of Collaborative Expertise" (London: Pearson, 2015).

Collaborative Cross-Sector Partnerships as a Strategy for Designing and Scaling Quality Education for All Young People in the 21st Century

Connie K. Chung, Associate Director,
Global Education Innovation Initiative, Harvard Graduate School of Education

How to organize and build strategic systemic and systematic partnerships as a way to design, scale, and spread good practices in public education

There is an old Korean proverb[4] that says, "Even a piece of blank paper is lighter when two people hold it together." As I have been thinking about the challenge of scaling good practice in public education to achieve quality education for all in the 21st century, I wonder if the field of education is not ripe for a systemic and systematic collaborative approach to addressing issues that seems to have eluded the attempts of many people and organizations operating independently.

I arrived at this thought from a couple of different angles. I have worked in the field of education as a teacher, consultant, and researcher to schools, districts, non-governmental organizations, and more recently, have focused specifically on thinking about the challenge of providing quality education for all in the 21st century as part of my research and work at the Global Education Innovation Initiative at the Harvard Graduate School of Education. For my doctoral dissertation, I studied the Greater Boston Interfaith Organization (GBIO), a citizens' collective in Massachusetts that was instrumental in identifying and leveraging the collective power of individuals and organizations to provide health care for all in Massachusetts in 2006 when they helped to pass a landmark bill in the state. Massachusetts' healthcare model became one for the country when President Obama signed into law the Affordable Care Act. I am drawing on both my experiences in education and my study of GBIO when I write this essay.

---

[4]백지장도 맞들면 낫다

1. Identify and work with people with a sense of agency and urgency, who know different parts of the education "elephant," and who share a common sense of purpose.

When I interviewed community leaders who were largely responsible for how Massachusetts was able to adopt a health care reform that successfully covered approximately two-thirds of the state's then-uninsured residents, they had several experiences in common:

(a) They knew that history had been shaped by individual choices; they personally knew people in their lives— usually parents or other mentors—who cared about their community and made a difference. Thus, they had a sense of agency, rooted in examples from history and from their own experiences, that they could use to shape the future, and in particular, their immediate communities.

(b) They all had attempted to solve "the healthcare problem" in individual ways—as doctors treating patients; as pastors and rabbis counseling people with long-term health and economic issues; as elected politicians and policymakers, listening to constituents' stories of unaffordable care; and as family members and friends listening to stories of those who had faced unexpected illnesses and had to navigate their way through a complex and debilitatingly expensive and ineffective system. They were invested in solving their shared problem and they shared a sense of urgency.

In conversation with each other, they listened to each other, and learned that they all wanted the same goal of improving access to affordable and quality health care in Massachusetts. They decided to work together to leverage their collective knowledge, human capital, and social capital to solve a problem that touched them all.

Their individual insights into the different aspects of the problem enabled them to design solutions that were more powerful than if they had worked on it alone. They were the proverbial blind men who were touching different parts of the elephant, thinking they were touching different animals, but in fact, had a profound grasp on different parts of the same animal or problem. Together, they fundamentally changed the health care system in Massachusetts.

Similarly, in education, at least in the United States, very few people who are touching the various parts of the education "elephant" have regular, systemic, and systematic means by which to speak with, listen to, learn from, and collaborate with each other. Various groups of people touching various different parts of the elephant that compose the experiences of young people as they grow up—teachers, parents, teacher education leaders, policymakers, researchers, service providers, after school programs, health care providers, social service providers, education material vendors, etc.—may speak within their group, but rarely does a district superintendent have a systemic or systematic means by which to speak with student teacher mentors, students, local teacher education institutions, and his state policymaker, for example.

Paul Dakin, an award-winning former superintendent of Revere, Massachusetts, may well be the exception: he brought together teachers from his surrounding five districts together to align their math curriculum and learn from each other. This was an initiative made possible, in part, only after speaking with students, teachers, parents, and other districts leaders. Through them, Dakin discovered how many of the students within those five neighboring school districts frequently changed schools due to family circumstances. They landed in math classes covering different parts of the curriculum, depending on the time of the year. In addition, he had found that because of the small size of the districts, math teachers had few opportunities to share good practices with others teaching the same topic.

2. Listen to each other and do the research to find shared, practical, systemic solutions.

It is notable that Dakin's approach to providing access to higher quality math education to students in Massachusetts differed from simple solutions such as changing the curriculum or hiring more math teachers. Rather, it was an orchestration made possible only by listening to various constituents of the education system, doing further research about the particular nature and specific scope of the issue (high student mobility within a specific number of districts, non-alignment of math curriculum across districts, non-sharing of best practices among teachers teaching the same topics), and then working together to find a common, practical systemic solution helpful to districts, teachers, and students alike.

Similarly, one of the member-leaders of the Boston-based community organization I interviewed shared a powerful metaphor to explain how his engagement with finding systemic responses differed from how he traditionally engaged with solving community challenges. He noted that as a pastor, he felt as though he was always called in to rescue "bodies floating down the river," when congregants reported needing food assistance or a job, for example. After having to rescue so many bodies, he had to wonder, "Why were these bodies floating down the river?" —in other words, "Why was there such a chronic shortage of fresh produce? Why were so many of his congregants unemployed?" He began to wonder about how to "stop the injuries at the source" or address the root of the problem, often entrenched in systemic dysfunction.

In education, we have evidence of many "bodies floating down the river," viewed through the lens of various stakeholders in education. From the perspective of young people, we see that each year, almost one third of all public high school students—and nearly one half all African Americans, Hispanics, and Native Americans students—fail to graduate from public high school on time with their classes.[5] From the teachers' perspectives, they report low satisfaction with their work and as a profession suffer a high rate of turnover, costing school districts upwards of $2.2 billion.[6] The economy, which is foundational to our quality of life, is undergoing rapid shifts in what some call the "fourth industrial revolution," so that we need to be mindful of not just equipping individual young people for life, but to also speaking with policymakers in other arenas to make sure that widening inequality and the rapid digitization that will change how we live, work, and relate to one another[7]—do not outstrip our humanity.

The call to find systemic and systematic solutions is an imperative, because to my mind, many of the lasting good practices in education are not silver bullets but instead are integrated in their approach and

---

[5] https://docs.gatesfoundation.org/Documents/TheSilentEpidemic3-06Final.pdf
[6] http://www.npr.org/sections/ed/2015/03/30/395322012/the-hidden-costs-of-teacher-turnover
[7] https://www.weforum.org/agenda/2016/01/the-fourth-industrial-revolution-what-it-means-and- how-to-respond/

scope. For example, merely identifying good teachers is not enough; good teachers need good schools where they are supported and respected, with a culture and support system that encourages continual learning and growth. These kinds of organizational cultures and systems rarely happen without good principals and district leaders with clear vision, and a policy environment that encourages learning and growth, in addition to accountability measures.

We also need new tools to facilitate the scaling and spreading of good practices, and while technology entrepreneurs are inventing them by the dozen, those who are able to speak with and learn from and work with educators are most likely to build ones that last. The best educational tools are co-constructed, used and tested in schools, and refined.[8] Empathy, that bedrock of design thinking, is better if empathy is not just imagined empathy, but felt empathy that comes from listening, visiting, experiencing, and knowing each others' challenges, values, and priorities.

3. Cultivate leaders and teachers who think systematically, systemically, and collaboratively about ways to develop the whole child.

Dakin did not just listen to various stakeholders and investigate various aspects of the issue of high student mobility and non-alignment of curriculum across districts, but formed a team to find common solutions. In my research about how to bring people from different backgrounds—ethnic, faith, socio-economic, and professional—together, I found that participants told me again and again about the value of working together across these differences on common projects that helped them to not only produce solutions that were grounded and achievable, but how the shared experience helped them to build relationships on which they could then build other projects.

To build the kinds of human-centered systems that offer quality education to more young people, we will need leaders who can think ethically, strategically, holistically, interconnectedly, relationally, and purposefully. Intentionally cultivating leaders with smaller egos who can

---

[8] Richard Rowe from the MIT Open Learning Exchange gave a wonderful presentation to this effect at the Harvard Advanced Leadership Institute's annual education think tank, in March 2016.

co-construct a greater sense of shared common purpose, and who can develop cultures and environments where trust can be exercised and built, may be another longer-term strategy to build the infrastructure from which to build, share, and spread good practice.

Leadership programs that do not just pass on knowledge, but also build time for reflection, for learning from what has been tried before and what is currently successful, for talking and listening to education stakeholders across the sector, including to one another, students, parents, teachers, and to mentors—may be a critical component in building systemic approaches to solving shared challenges. In my interviews with the leaders of GBIO—many of whom had graduate degrees in law, medicine, health, education, or theology—told me that until they joined GBIO, they had not had the opportunity to learn the particular skills they needed about how to work with others to trigger and achieve systemic change.

The opportunity to not just think and write, but to engage in the practical work of collaborating with others "not like them" – neither in political views nor professional skills – but who share a common purpose – and to iterate practical real-life solutions may be another important aspect to consider. Many such small programs exist, such as in Singapore's Principal Leadership Education Program, but perhaps not at scale, nor connected with each other, even as the world shrinks.

While on-going teacher professional development may be another way to improve quality in education, it is more difficult to persuade people to change behavior mid- stream. A focus on developing pre-service teacher programs to incorporate frameworks for professional standards of behavior that incorporates as must-have's, principles such as continual learning, reflective professional development, ways of thinking that intentionally focuses on considering the purposes of education, systemic ways of thinking, and collaboration – may be helpful as much as a focus on curriculum and pedagogy. Cultivating in teachers at the beginning of their induction into the profession, the kinds of skills and competencies they will need to be part of a collaborative approach to addressing the various needs of developing the whole child for the 21st century may well be a challenge that teacher education institutions would do well to take up.

A few wonderings:

I close this essay with a few wonderings that flow from these thoughts: (a) Do we need a sector within education whose primary job is to identify and bring together the people and organizations necessary to document, share, and help implement good practices within and across education systems?

It appears that very few education systems have directed human and financial resources to bringing together people to work with each other to identify, curate, document, share, and co-create good education practices and approaches. By contrast, we have many reports issued by single organizations on good practices. Yet even when these documents exist, they may not be written or presented in a way that would help organizations execute, implement, monitor to tweak these good practices.

It may be a people-centered endeavor—indeed, it may require an effort to organize people and organizations—as well as ideas—that may be the innovation we have not yet tried. Tony Bryk has pioneered thinking in this work with his colleagues on networked improvement communities, but I wonder if there might not also be ways to systematically incorporate such ways of being, learning, and collaborating within and across systems more intentionally and deliberately.

(b) Might foundations and other funders work not only to fund programs and host conferences, but also to build ecosystems for projects, programs, and people who are working on related issues and encouraging them to work together?

Very few people have the opportunity to gain a birds-eye view of the multiple smaller projects that are happening in various parts of the world. Foundations and funders, however, may have a better sense than most. Might they play a more intentional role in linking the people and organizations that are working on similar aspects of the education elephant, and encourage them to work together? The Hewlett Foundation's work in Deeper Learning may be one example. The Ford Foundation's work in K-12 civic education in the United

States, may be another. Similarly are there lessons to be learned and shared across different stakeholders working on similar issues?

In other words, might we create more explicit neighborhood, city, regional, national, and global education networks to leverage our collective knowledge to co-create the conditions in which we can achieve our shared desire to equip and incline young people to have the knowledge, skills, values and attitudes to co-create a more just, caring, and sustainable world together? Our shared future may well depend on it.

Connie K. Chung *is the Associate Director of the Global Education Innovation Initiative at the Harvard Graduate School of Education. She is the co-editor of the book, Teaching and Learning for the Twenty-First Century: Educational Goals, Policies, and Curricula from Six Nations (Harvard Education Press, 2016), a co-author of the curriculum resource, Empowering Global Citizens: A World Course (CreateSpace Independent Publishing Platform, 2016), and a contributor to a book about education improvement efforts in the United States, A Match on Dry Grass: Community Organizing as a Catalyst for School Reform (Oxford University Press, 2011).*

The renewal of school culture
Armando Estrada, Co Founder and Executive Director, Vía Educación

More than ever, the challenges of our society demand radical changes in the way we educate:

- What would a school have to do to incorporate in the best possible way the changes necessary to transform education, as a whole?

- How to ensure that educational reforms cover real cultural changes, are interdisciplinary and multi-sectorial, in order to place education as the priority on every stakeholder's agenda?

- What should we in the international arena do to cultivate disruptive supra-national efforts so that we may engage effectively in the educational reforms of entire regions and continents?

- What are the enablers of change that make society see the need for technically-competent and socially-valuable educational processes?

It is disturbing see how we as a society are constantly challenging the limits of coexistence, participation, and justice. Tragically, live examples of the human-diminishing way we educate are becoming more frequently repeated in the media. Societal and environmental issues bear the common threads of greed and selfishness. Problems such as inequality, profound loneliness, pollution, and climate change have the same root cause: a dysfunctional education system that fails to adequately prepare people for life in the 21st century.

Why despite of all our efforts our societies keep failing to address what is needed to address these challenges?

Of course, we know education is the answer; however, we continue designing reforms and programs to put additional pressure on teachers and schools, and then we leave them alone, thinking that we were clear about what we need from them, and then waiting to blame others for what did not produce the desired result.

The 21st century competencies our children and youth urgently need to reorganize society to be more humane and to protect our ecosystem must not be just another intention or a task on teachers' to-do lists. True educational reform will only happen when every actor in society is able to see its part in the job, when each one performs and celebrates, and leads others by example who have not decided yet to do the same.

Why do corporations—which demand honest, empathetic, self-directed collaborators, willing to take risks and make decisions—not use more of their creative, technical, and financial capacities to understand the complexities of schools? Where would their talent come from if not from evolved schools and mature communities of citizens? Why do they offer products and services that might be good in the short term but put the future at risk? Where does this disconnection come from?

We usually see ourselves as apart from the problem and therefore we are far from the solution. We believe that there is always someone else who is responsible.

Why does innovation in education promoted by universities and research centers take so long to be systematized and replicated? Why don't good projects get implemented, and, on the contrary, do they stay as research initiatives that never achieve reality? Is it because sometimes researchers assume the role of observers of realities, but they do not care to transform that reality?

Why do practitioners' organizations, who have the power to bring new practices and processes to achieve greater results in schools, work in isolation and with very low impact? Is it because there is a great will to implement solutions, but only when they are able to apply their own idea? Does their ego prevent them from assuming new roles and becoming more effective in working within systemic networks?

Why do governments, which are responsible for decision making on educational policies, get in trouble when education innovations are not politically correct for the groups and associations they represent? Is it because they generally don't consider themselves as conveners of change, and they don't fully recognize that their power comes from their ability to integrate voices, bringing together the best experiences to try, adapt, and replicate? Educational authorities in government generally have been closed to these collaborative spaces and co-designing solutions. They typically have failed to understand the needs of all schools in their systems and to integrate multi-sectorial alliances to meet the requirements in every community.

The importance of acquiring the skills needed for success in the 21st century does not lie in the "what" but in the "how." The "how" involves giving the opportunity to play to those who have not traditionally been able to participate, or those who should be allowed to participate in a more active way—taking on roles as stewards, not only as providers or observers; as guardians of a shared vision in education and accountable for the end results that emerge.

At this point in history, these "how's" can shape the future, and if we are not careful enough, we could fail yet again. We must avoid thinking that the transformation in education must come from one person (the teacher) and one institution (the school). We run the risk of thinking of wonderful, new ideas about what we want, and then mistakenly delegating this transformation to someone else.

Three interrelated elements

Thus, there are three interrelated elements that may help 21st century skills become a profound and enduring reality, and not just another subject in the curriculum that will, despite a good attempt to genuinely bring these skills to play, fail systemically at developing the desired skills:

Co-responsibility

Co-responsibility is our sense of identity as educators, whatever our status or role is. From individuals or institutions, co-responsibility means the ability to honor our capacity to form and influence others, especially children and adolescents. It is our ability to identify ourselves as part of the problem, as well as part of the solution—and of monitoring others do their fair share too.

When a sense of shared responsibility is placed in the center of our work, the weight of the task at hand will be lighter, no matter how complex it seems, because it will be no longer the task of a single individual but of many, even thousands. Thus, it is vital that co-responsibility must be demonstrated in our efforts and made explicit to all stakeholders. On the other hand, denying responsibility is serious: this is why we need self-control mechanisms and incentives that are aligned to a sense of collaboration; this is why it is necessary to have a social movement in place.

A social movement

When we think that great educational transformation is only in the hands of teachers and school members, we are underestimating the potential of society to transform itself. We need to renew our lenses and see new ways to educate. We must ask the whole society to recognize its role to educate the whole child.

If we want to equip society with the kinds of competencies needed for the new era, we have to engage and sustain a mobilization of every agent of society to step in and play its role in educating the children and the community around them. Social movements are an effective way of achieving transformation. They also help to norm our behavior and to give us more and better ideas of how to pick ourselves up when we fail.

Social movements are effective because they make change possible, not through control or the exercise of power, but because they have the ability to influence. It is through freedom and self-consciousness where one can achieve enduring results both at the individual and collective level. Social movements have demonstrated they are able to move the needle on a consensus on the fundamental rights of some groups, have been successful in changing trends in the consumption of certain products and services, and they have connected people through technology. It is necessary to encourage a supra-national trend, linked to national and local movements to redefine the role of education and enhance its social value through co-responsibility. One could say, we need a movement for the "Renewal of School Culture."School culture is intangible but it exists. It dictates the way we act and the decisions we make. It guides our interactions and shapes our commitments. It

66

connects or divides us in terms of shared goals. It gives us a sense of belonging and rootedness.

A Systemic perspective

This renewed educational culture requires a systemic approach to be effective. That is, taking into account not only every actor, but the relations among them, the flow of information and decision-making between them, including their level of commitment. The systemic perspective aims to build a shared vision of success and to develop the skills and knowledge necessary to achieve it. It is able to detect when additional capabilities are needed to meet new demands and avoid going obsolete. Above all, it is able to build bridges between different actors and identify leverage points where the contribution of stakeholders is essential. A concrete example of shared responsibility as a social movement with a systemic perspective is working on projects for the renewal of the school culture at a district level.

Why start the movement at the district level, you might ask?

Initiatives working with all schools in a district for a reasonable period of time can influence the way teachers and educational actors work, the way students learn, and the way parents and community participate.

Educational initiatives, research, and even school reforms often conclude that more professional development for teachers is what is most required. However, teachers might receive exceptional training opportunities but when they close the door of their classroom, it often takes just a matter of weeks or days for the prevailing school culture and policy climate to dissolve every teacher's intention to change unless, there is a principal who supports, accompanies, advises, and helps define a course of action together with teachers. But, the principal might also fail to do this unless she or he has a supervisor who gives good advice, is willing to spend time figuring out a specific case, is able to try different alternatives, is able to analyze and assess information, and can create different scenarios. But, even a good supervisor is subject to failure when a toxic culture is in place. Unless there is a superintendent who is clear about the kinds of key educational challenges the schools are facing and is committed to transforming the community that was conferred to her through the power of quality education.

This same paradigm touches even the Ministry of Education where, when there is a clear understanding, are specific strategies to meet those needs, and there is the will to invest the right amount of time in developing the right school culture, education can fulfill its most important purpose. Any other paradigm will fall short in achieving it.

For the renewal of school culture, it is essential to have the parents and the community involved so they may become active and proactive participants in the school culture. Thriving parents and allies who organize can create a sustainable community for the school. They will continue to participate because they feel the school is a welcoming space for collective development and because they see their role in that vision.

In addition, corporations should value education more intensively and actively. They must realize that education happens in school, but also at home, on public transportation, in advertisements and television programs, and in the goods and products they sell. As such, corporations should be willing to be part the movement a high quality, relevant 21st century education.

The stakes are high: if we fail to achieve a social movement with a systemic approach to engage in a renewal of the school culture, we are seriously putting at stake our present and future as humanity.

When there is this convergence between actors and commitment, it is easy to imagine an educational system capable of meeting the challenges of any school in any environment, to understand how the whole community can serve as co-educator, to make bold structural changes in our school reforms, to develop the mastery of teachers, and to increase in multiple ways the collaboration between schools and parents. This is important because an education that is relevant and is able to form its citizens with the skills needed to innovate and evolve is not the task of a single person or institution. Change in education must come from multiple actors and forces that are aware of their collective capacity.

What is at stake is so precious, it ultimately defines our role on this little blue planet of ours.

Armando Estrada is co-founder and executive director at Via Educacion, an organization based in Mexico that seeks to promote opportunities for sustainable social development through education; it accomplishes its mission through the design, implementation, evaluation and dissemination of education initiatives for citizenship engagement. He is member of the Academy for Systems Change and fellow of Ashoka, an global network of social entrepreneurs.

Developing 21st century skills through higher education

María Figueroa, Dean of the Education Faculty at Universidad Externado, Colombia.
Felipe Martínez, Adjunct Professor of the Education Faculty, Universidad Externado, Colombia

In what ways do various organizations support 21st century education? What scale have they reached?

Universidad Externado in Colombia works to develop 21st century skills at two levels: directly with teachers working in schools, and, at a more global level, working indirectly with teachers.

The direct work with teachers that focuses on developing these skills occurs through formal master's programs offered by the Faculty of Education. In 2016, a new master's program was created, with an emphasis on specific skills areas. This program aims to have teachers acquire the necessary skills so that the students they teach can be competitive and can transform their environment. The competencies master's students will develop include 21st century skills—understood in this context as the skill that teachers need to have to solve problems, communicate effectively, work in teams, critical and quantitative thinking, and understand their environment and their profession while being critical and creative. Generic skills have been developed, in several classes, in a transversal way across the curriculum. For example, including reflections about their own practice and their own learning processes as well as the analyses of their institution standardized tests results, or the diagnostic of their institution in terms of their needs. Currently this master's program has 171 students that teach approximately 19,500 students.

Another way in which Externado is working to promote 21st century skills is through training future teachers that are participating in the Teach for Colombia program. This program selects excellent young graduates from recognized universities, provides basic teacher training, and then assigns them to teach at low-income schools throughout Colombia for two years. Among the topics of the future teachers' initial preparation, the training focuses on pedagogical skills, but also leadership, context-aware teaching, and communication skills. These

71

skills later will affect the way in which more than 19,850 students are taught.

The direct work done by Externado with teachers is contributing to changing the perception of what being a teacher means by developing these skills and their scaling.

The second level at which Externado develops 21st century skills is by focusing indirectly on teachers, through its leadership in teacher assessment and evaluation processes, and in the preparation of new teachers. In these cases, teacher evaluation systems, for both K-12 teachers and university professors, are being developed and constructed with the participation of Externado. A team of Externado faculty members was hired by the Ministry of Education of Colombia to consult on the development of the new K-12 teacher evaluation process. This has been a hot topic with teacher unions in the country, and the final version of the evaluation now includes some aspects that will make teachers reflect about their practice and about what skills they are developing in students. Even though Colombia's educational policies have not stated a clear position on the development of 21st century competences, there is indirect reference to these skills, such as references to the development of critical thinking. There is still much work to be done in helping teachers develop 21st century skills, as well as teaching them to students, but teacher assessment is one of the channels that can help teachers be more aware of the importance of these skills in their practice.

Externado is also involved in analyzing and establishing a new ways to evaluate university faculty. Even though there is more momentum to incorporate 21st century skills in K-12 education, university teaching is frequently still focused on more traditional learning—focused on content mastery. The REDES group (Red de Evaluación De la Educación Superior) was created with the purpose of generating systematic reflection on the different ways in which university teachers are evaluated. This network is made up by professionals, teachers, and researchers from ten universities in Colombia.

REDES has met monthly starting in February 2016 to discuss the definition of a framework of good teaching at the university level and the development of valid instruments to carry out that evaluation.

Reflection and evaluation of good teaching in universities requires establishing specific criteria where university teachers are explicitly developing 21st century skills in their students. A few examples of these criteria, which are also considered in the evaluation instrument, include the development of critical thinking and collaborative work skills in the university classroom.

Externado University is also contributing to developing 21st century skills by exerting influence on national public policy, specifically on the creation of the laws that guide the faculties of education nationwide. *Resolution 02041* of 2016 was developed by a team of professionals that included several faculty members from Externado. This resolution establishes the specific characteristics related to quality for teacher preparation programs in Colombia, including how these programs can be accredited by the government. The new law proposes, among other things, more practical training for potential teachers, and research in the classrooms as part of undergraduate teacher preparation programs. There are also some specific components that should be incorporated into the curriculum of such programs, including the development of general skills such as reading, quantitative reasoning, and English as a second language. Additionally, this resolution provides guidance as to specific content and skills that teachers need to receive before starting their professional work.

What protocols, tools, processes, and systems are used by those organizations to support effective practices of 21st century education?

In Colombia we have identified some resources and protocols that could be used in developing and scaling 21st century competences. An important tool to do so is the GRIT scale (Duckworth & Quinn, 2009), which can be used to assess some skills that belong within the 21st century competency framework. The GRIT scale measures resilience, perseverance, motivation, and organization. With a reliable measurement of grit, teachers can begin to identify whether their practice is helping to develop this skill in their students. The scale has also been used by some universities in order to correlate its results with students' performance, and have started exploring if it is possible to use it as a predictor of specific contexts.

On the other hand, a group of educators in Colombia has also been collaborating with an international expert named Koji Miyamoto on socio-emotional skills. Dr. Miyamoto has had several meetings with NGOs and government officials to help increase awareness of the importance of these skills. From these meetings, education stakeholders in Colombia have learned more about social and emotional skills. Some of the education sector's key actors now know the kind of activities that could lead to the strengthening of social and emotional skills, which are an important part of the 21st century competences. Dr. Miyamoto has also emphasized understanding the social context of Colombia in order to develop discussions and reflections in class with the guidance of teachers in order to develop social and emotional skills.

Some schools in Colombia are developing teaching models that develop 21st century skills. For example, a group of charter schools in Bogotá, Asociación Alianza Educativa, and some private schools have been developing, with the goal of improving academic achievement and interpersonal skills, cooperative learning strategies in all areas of knowledge. The model is not perfect, and there have been difficulties in sharing these experiences with other schools, but the existence of this knowledge is a step in the direction of developing methods to foster 21st century competences.

In summary, there are few formal instruments in place to measure the effectiveness of teaching 21st century skills in Colombia and via Externado. This is an area that can definitely grow in the future and could benefit from the results of collaborations like those facilitated through the Global Education Innovation Initiative Think Tank.

What barriers do those organizations face to further scaling their impact, serving more children?

One of the big barriers to scaling is the lack of follow-up on curricula that develop 21st century skills. For example, several programs in the Faculty of Education of Externado are focused on developing global education competencies. For example, there are courses focused on communicative competencies; however, there are no specific follow—up protocols or tools that have been developed for measuring the skills developed in those courses. Yet, there are concrete assessment activities that measure students' development in related areas, including written projects and oral defenses among others. Additionally, there are no teacher evaluations that focus specifically on 21st century skills. Even though there are efforts in the country to change these evaluations (such as the changes incorporated into the national teacher's evaluation) these assessment processes have yet to incorporate the 21st century skills explicitly.

Another limitation is that subject-based learning drives the curriculum and, even though we know the correlation between cognitive skills and non-cognitive skills is high, in many educational discussions the priority is still developing basic language and math skills. Very little focus is given to 21st century education, perhaps because of the lack of knowledge and practice among teachers in developing these skills.

Other barriers are directly related to the greater educational community. Traditional education, overall, is still undervalued in many segments of the population, which leads to high student dropouts rates in both K-12 education (4.86% in 2010) and universities (45.3% in 2014) (Ministry of Education, 2010, 2014). Perhaps students leave the educational system because the curriculum lacks real life learning opportunities that include 21st century skills. The real fact is, that if students are not part of the education system and do not have significant guidance or support in their learning process out of school, they won't have access to learning these and other skills.

A significant barrier exists in the form of the quality of teachers in Colombia. In many cases, these teachers have not developed 21st century skills themselves, which makes it more challenging for them to teach skills such as collaboration and critical thinking to their students.

Another important barrier that Colombia should address before improving its education system is the antagonistic relationship between teachers, and the government.

In addition, there are many 21st century skills that are not traditionally part of the Colombian culture. Therefore, little attention is paid at school or at home to the development of these skills. One area of improvement can be in how to make these skills more explicit so that both parents and teachers can work together in teaching them to children. Many parents in low-income conditions have their children unplanned, have not themselves completed the formal education cycle, and need to work two jobs in order to be able to sustain their families. When speaking with teachers and principals in focus groups, one their most common complaints is that some parents consider the schools "parking lots for their children." In sum, many parents do not have the skills, the interest, or the time to support their children's education, including in terms of the development of their 21st century skills.

What would be necessary to support scaling of 21st century education practices? What processes, protocols, tools, and systems would enable such scaling?

Colombia, as a country, has recently tried to foster 21st century competences in all of its school-age population. Given the greater social context and the recent peace agreement between the government and guerrilla groups (which is still under negotiation), Colombia is promoting a generalized program called *Cátedra de la Paz* (Teaching for Peace). The Teaching for Peace law states that schools and universities must devote some time to teaching Colombian students to better create a culture for peace. Within the Teaching for Peace framework, students must work on at least two of the following topics: justice and human rights; sustainable use of natural resources; protection of the cultural and natural wealth of the nation; peaceful conflict resolution; bullying prevention; diversity; political participation; historic memory; moral dilemmas; social impact projects; history of national and international peace agreements; life project planning; and risk prevention. We consider this a very valuable initiative that could be improved to scale some 21st century competences.

The national government also has recently promoted the National Center for Historic Memory. This center is collecting all of the written, oral, and other-format accounts of victims of the protracted armed conflict. The National Center for Historic Memory recently released a tool which narrates some of these stories, and makes suggestions on how to use them in the classroom. We believe that the existence of this information and legislation is a step in the right direction towards promoting some of the most urgent 21st century skills.

We also recognize that these two strategies on their own do not suffice in order to promote 21st century competences throughout the whole country. There are several barriers as mentioned above that our society still need to deal with in order to better promote these skills.

As noted above, one important barrier that must be overcome in order to develop 21st century skills is evaluation and measurement. In Colombia, ICFES (Instituto Colombiano para la Evaluación de la Educación) has made efforts to measure factors associated with academic performance through surveys. Among these factors are several 21st century competences and skills. This results of this assessment are used to indicate school quality on the Synthetic Index of School Quality, a country-wide measurement developed taking in consideration four aspects: performance in Saber test (the national standardized test), improvement in Saber test, school efficiency (percentage of students promoted to the next grade), and school environment. However, on several attempts to use the results, researchers have found that most of this data is not very useful; since 80% of it is based on Saber tests, information already known, and the 10% based on school environment does not have a relevant variability.

Evaluation institutes should start to include simple questions on their national assessments that focus on 21st century skills and global education competencies. It would also be very important to have performance assessments that include real world situations on national and international standardized exams. PISA (the Program for International Student Assessment) has undertaken the challenge of measuring some of these competences, but more effort at a national and international level needs to be expended. Even though it may not be possible to include all competences on PISA, one initial approach can be to undertake an analysis of how these skills are related among each other and how they are related to cognitive skills. In this way, assessments can include the most reliable and valid measurement of these skills.

These assessments also can include a formative component, where students can receive feedback on their performance and teachers can identify what gaps their students need to continue developing. Professional development for teachers should also be a priority so teachers can develop 21st century skills and know how to teach them to students. We also believe that a strategy could include incorporating 21st century skills in a more explicit manner within the teacher evaluation process (both K-12 and at the university level) in Colombia. Gathering information about the level of skill teachers have as well as their ability to teach these skills can help in designing new strategies to scale at a national level.

Next, to foster 21st century competences, it is important to help parents to support their children in their education process. Creating a more inclusive and friendly environment between teachers and government officials could promote further collaboration among schools and communities to provide better education for Colombian children. In a similar way, we need to use different methods to promote and build support for 21st century skills including, parents, social media, and traditional media. The more explicit the communication about the importance of these skills, the higher the national priority will be to embrace them into formal and non-formal educational policies.

Finally, we need to share and highlight how organizations are using 21st century skills to promote these same skills. Examples of this include initiatives that generate global collaboration with groups such as the Global Education Innovation Initiative and Global Connections.

María Figueroa is the Dean of the Education Faculty at the Universidad Externado de Colombia. She has participated as advisor for several institutions such as Icfes (Colombian Institution for Education Evaluation) and the Ministry of Education. Her interests are assessment of different subjects areas, teacher evaluation, and evaluation of generic skills.

Luis Felipe Martínez is an education consultant at the World Bank Group in Colombia and adjunt professor at Universidad Externado de Colombia. He is interested and has experience in education research and education policy analysis. Passionate admirer of teachers and their contribution to our society.

References:

Duckworth, A. L., & Quinn, P. D. (2009). Development and Validation of the Short Grit Scale (Grit–S). *Journal of Personality Assessment, 91*(2), 166–174.

Ministerio de Educación Nacional. (2010). Plan Sectorial 2010 2014. Bogotá, Colombia: Ministerio de Educación Nacional.

Ministerio de Educación Nacional. (2015). Guía para la Implementación del modelo de Gestión de Permanencia y Graduación Estudiantil en Instituciones de Educación Superior. Bogotá, Colombia: Ministerio de Educación Nacional.

Changing Science Teaching Practice in Chile.

Paulina Grino, MA Teacher and Teaching Education, ECBI –Chile, University of Chile.

The general goal for 21st education is to prepare students for 21st century needs by providing cognitive, intrapersonal, and interpersonal competencies. Educational organizations have currently taken on the role of supporting school stakeholders in preparing students with these competencies from different perspectives and standpoints. The question left to answer is, then how do these educational organizations support 21st century education? In this essay, I attempt to answer this question from the organization I represent, which provides inquiry-based science education by working with classroom teachers and student in schools from K to 12. In addition, I present tools and processes that serve 21st century education. In a third part, I include some of the barriers the program faces for scaling and reaching more teachers and students. Finally, I reflect about what is necessary to support 21st century education.

ECBI program and its role in 21st century education

The program Educacion en Ciencias Basado en Indagacion ECBI (Inquiry-based Science Education) located in Chile, provides professional development mainly for classroom teachers focused on science content and inquiry as pedagogy inquiry as pedagogy. With fifteen years of experience, this program, based at the Universidad de Chile, has worked with governmental support as well as with private and local funding sources to implement its programs throughout the country. ECBI works directly in schools developing plans of action depending on community educational vision or single school's reality and context. Specifically, ECBI has established the idea of professional development pathway support with a facilitator to work one-on-one with teachers. This facilitator is an expert in inquiry pedagogy, and assists in lesson planning and curriculum enactment and the reflection of the teacher´s practices. Some of the success stories of our program are the product of school principal and administrative personnel involvement as well as a strong relationship between the facilitator and classroom teacher, among other factors.

Specifically, ECBI-facilitators develop science-related competencies with teachers and students within the school environment. Typically, elementary school teachers do not feel confident with regards to science content and tend to use traditional pedagogies to teach this subject matter. ECBI works in developing the understanding of science and inquiry pedagogy with teachers to plan and enact science lessons that place students at the center of their learning. In this way, ECBI supports 21st century education by providing equitable access through science learning opportunities to classroom teachers and students.

From my perspective and considering ECBI's plan of action, educational organizations can support 21st century learning by providing competencies that have not been otherwise acquired or developed. For example, ECBI brings science into schools through more innovative pedagogies which are not necessarily the focus of teachers and/or school directive and administrative personnel specially in this era of high stakes testing where the focus has been on improving test scores rather than improving teaching and learning. In this sense, educational organizations can provide opportunities that have not been provided by other stakeholders and that are required to implement 21st education priorities.

ECBI, in particular, works directly with teachers and students; however we believe that a stronger approach to changing today's science education is by involving whole communities. This requires strengthening the sense of responsibility of school communities and school institutional educational projects. Therefore, educational organizations can support 21st century education by working with and supporting the role of each stakeholder in a school and community.

ECBI's tools and processes to support 21st century education

ECBI implements plans of action that are developed according to the needs of each school it partners with. In order to undertake this work, ECBI facilitators become involved in the school culture, plan opportunities for professional development, plan science lessons, coach teachers while in the classroom, and perform assessment for learning approach to make progress. Since ECBI works with different schools that differ socially and culturally, the barriers and opportunities to develop our work vary. The protocols and processes we use are highly dependent on the particular schools and their context; however, we typically use classroom observation protocols, teacher self-evaluations, student's perceptions, and principal perceptions of the implementation process among other tools.

Another important part of our protocol and processes is in relation to science curriculum. Since ECBI works mainly with preschools, elementary, and middle schools, facilitators must study and fully understand the national curriculum along with the grade at which the teacher works and have been implementing such curriculum in classrooms, therefore the plan can put to in action in a progressive perspective. In order to provide opportunities for science education in our country, our protocols and processes need to follow and enrich this national science curriculum, with the support and input of teachers and students.

It is important to also think about the need to develop a trust relationship with teachers in order to be able to work with them within their classroom, and to truly develop the abilities we are attempting to develop. The relationship between facilitator and teacher is another fundamental part and process of this program.

In summary, the specific process and protocol we are highly dependent on the school ECBI is working with. Some of the protocols we currently use are related to the perception of principal and students in regard to the implementation of our program, in addition to teacher self-assessment and protocols for classroom observation. General aspects of these processes include: (1) connecting with national standards and curriculum and their enactment in the classroom and (2) building meaningful relationship with teachers that allow facilitators to work with them in their classrooms.

The barriers: ECBI's challenges to scale

From my perspective, national standards, curriculum, and assessment of teachers and students represent important barriers to scaling and serving more students. The requirements established by the Chilean Minister of Education are considerable in terms of paperwork and related tasks that, in the end, make schools' personnel work attending to administrative issues rather than finding innovative pedagogies to support student learning. School principal and other related personnel, in particular, often find themselves on the perimeter of the learning process and not necessarily supporting teachers in their practice.

Another aspect that represents a barrier for scaling is related to the national standards and curriculum itself. From my perspective, the national science standards and curriculum are highly focused on content rather than scientific skills or positive attitudes to science. We recognize and appreciate the need for developing such skills and attitudes, but the Chilean national science curriculum enactment and assessment fails to do so resulting on teachers presenting science content rather than involving students in learning to do science. In addition, since teacher performance in Chile is assessed based on how students perform on standards evaluations, and these results impact a teacher's career, their focus is therefore almost entirely placed on content and the students passing such tests, rather than developing scientific reasoning.

Schools of education represent another layer for concern in scaling. As ECBI has been working and reaching more schools and teachers, we have learned that new teachers graduate lacking an appropriate science education and with knowing traditional approaches for teaching rather than current or more innovative approaches for teaching science. Thus, new teachers become another group, different from expert teachers, requiring different processes and protocols to lead to a change in their practice.

To summarize, the barriers that keep us from scaling are associated mainly with the our current education system including the national science curriculum and its accountability and evaluation processes that require the attention of teachers and school principals since it impacts their performance and ultimately their career as educators. The other main barrier is related to schools of education, in that they are traditional and less innovative institutions.

A topic that warrants discussion is question of scale. In the ECBI case, we think about the sustainability of the program in schools, and aim to avoid building a dependent relationship between the facilitator and the teacher. In order to do so, we look for leaders (teachers or other school stakeholders) that can take on the leadership of the program in the school after the facilitator goes to other school. In other words, we believe that scaling up will only happen by developing competencies in a team of teachers that they are able to use to continue this work and build a professional learning community. In this sense, a barrier to scaling that we face is that teachers we sometimes identify as leaders lack the deep science knowledge or are overwhelmed with administrative issues to keep the program vibrant, causing our efforts in that particular school to fade over time. What we propose is to assist the school in developing their own capacities instead of depending on an external to the school. This way, we are supporting schools and teachers in science teaching and learning in their own environment, rather than imposing a pedagogy and a model that could fail over time. In sum, teachers need to feel a sense of belonging with regards to this pedagogy—a sense that needs to be developed with time.

As a program with fifteen years of experience, we believe that as we scale, we need to ensure that teachers and students involved in this process fully understand the fundamental ideas of teaching science through inquiry-based pedagogies, so as not only to achieve the Ministery of Education requirements and pass content-related assessments, but also to provide equal access to high-quality science education and develop scientific skills for all students.

The needs: tools, protocols and systems to support 21st century education.

As noted above, making room for innovation seems one important path for supporting scaling. As the national standards and curriculum, along with standardized testing, are by all accounts rigid processes, schools and school systems that focus on them are not necessarily focused on looking for innovative teaching strategies. As a program we must support teachers to understand those results as evidence for progression and improvement of pedagogical practices.

In general, what is needed to support 21st century education is to re-think those aspects of the educational system that were designed under other contexts and circumstances. For example, rethinking how teaching has been conceptualized and practiced within school classrooms as an expositive way to transfer knowledge would support 21st century education. Thus, it is needed to target schools of education so that they graduate teachers that are prepared to find ways to teach every student. This requires us to think of three aspects of teacher education: (1) scientific and pedagogical knowledge (in the case of the work of ECBI); (2) pedagogical knowledge' for progression and (3) socio- and emotional skills.

Another aspect to consider is building a strategic educational project that involves the school community, allowing for stronger collaborations among schools and educational organizations. Finally, educational research could potentially serve scaling efforts by developing models and providing evidence that support innovative practice.

In sum, what is necessary for scaling is involvement and collaboration from all stakeholders in education, fully understanding their position and roles within the education system, with respect and accordance to their culture and values.

Paulina Grino works for Inquiry-based Science Education Program in Chile. She holds a Master degree in Teaching and Teacher Education and currently works on her dissertation which is focused on Science teaching among rural and indigenous schools.

Skills for the 21st century: Perspectives and contributions from the Active Urban School

Santiago Isaza Arango, Director of Education, Luker Foundation

Recently, I had the opportunity to discuss what young people in the 21st century need in terms of an education while at Harvard University, within the framework of the Global Education Innovation Initiative's Think Tank, led by Professor Fernando Reimers and other experts from different countries.

During the two-day meeting, we not only had the opportunity to analyze the transformations that traditional education paradigms should undertake, but also to reflect on the possibilities of scaling up initiatives that are already showing progress in these processes. In addition, there was discussion of what obstacles might exist to scale up and take a step towards a truly "21st century" education. In the different subgroups of work during the workshop, we were able to analyze—in a preliminary way—some models of scalability of the training of skills for the 21st century.

For my role as Director of Education at the Luker Foundation in Colombia, it was very important to have participated in this process of reflection and also to share an initiative that we have been developing for more than fourteen years, which we believe is contributing in some way to transforming "traditional" education in public schools into an educational approach with appropriate characteristics for the needs of the 21st century. This initiative is called "Active Urban School.", and fosters a better quality of education in the city of Manizales, through a whole school approach (K-11° and all the main subjects), incorporating active pedagogies[9], with a special emphasis in developing social and emotional skills on students. AUS is been implemented in the 55% of the public urban schools of the city.

In this brief letter, I want to express my reactions regarding the analysis mentioned above, and also to demonstrate somehow our experiences

---

[9] Based on the Escuela Nueva model, but adapted to the urban context.

with the Active Urban School model exemplify the general guidelines we have come up with for a 21st century education with global reach.

Different people have written about and made taxonomies on 21st century skills. I personally subscribe to the one made by the National Research Council, headed by James Pellegrino and Margaret Hilton (2012), that proposes a framework of competencies divided into the following three domains: cognitive, interpersonal, and intrapersonal. This framework does not leave aside the development of cognitive competencies, which are fundamental, but also adds competencies that a human being must have to be well with himself and with society in general.

Now, regarding the "what"—all of us who work in education can, perhaps, come to an agreement upon the competencies, such as those outlined by Pellegrino and Hilton (and when I refer to all, I speak of policymakers, teachers, teaching directors, parents, foundations, universities, etc).

However, in the "how" there may be much greater distances between opinions, and that is why the Global Education Innovation Initiative Think Tank has been convened: to think on how the experiences that have stood out in the different publications of this group and the others which can be highlighted at a global level can be replicated in a massive way. We have to put aside the "transmissionist" style of education, and instead give priority to an educational approach where our young people have greater empowerment and the opportunity for greater personal development.

The "Active Urban Schools" model

The Luker Foundation has been working since 2002 through a public, private, and academic alliance, made up mainly by the mayor of Manizales, Colombia's office, the Luker Foundation, the Cinde Foundation, and the University of Manizales. Together we have developed the Active Urban School program, which seeks to improve the quality of public education (K-11) through the implementation of an active pedagogical model that promotes academic, social, and emotional skills through the following principles: autonomy, participation, and socially-active learning. The model is inspired by

88

Escuela Nueva, a model of education developed in Colombia for rural schools, that has to date shown important results.

In this way, the Active Urban School model is a whole approach initiative in the school, transforming practices through the following tools:

(1) **Methodological process:** It starts by taking into account the *previous knowledge* of the students. Then the *theoretical and conceptual framework* of the subject in question is developed. Subsequently, an *exercise* phase is reached, where what is seen in the previous stage is put into practice. The process ends with the *application* in real life of the topic at hand. This process is referenced in guides and self-learning textbooks (textbooks that are developed by the students with the support of their teachers) for all of the fundamental topic areas of grades K to 11th. In addition, the teachers can adapt these materials or create their own.

(2) **Collaborative learning:** The program puts great emphasis on collaborative learning, which is why during the methodological process interaction among the students is encouraged. There is also a proposal regarding the physical distribution of the classroom, where classes are provided with hexagonal tables for teamwork among six students per table, instead of traditional uni-personal desks. Students collaborate with each other and the teacher facilitates the learning processes giving master classes in the moments that are necessary, but not during the whole class, as typically happens in the conventional educational model.

(3) **Student Government and Committees:** To develop leadership, responsibility, participation, and democratic behaviors in students, there is a deliberate student government strategy, where each student in the classroom has a democratically-elected role. For example, in each classroom, there is: a classroom president, vice-president, treasurer, and secretary, as well as leaders of recreation, journalism, health, and environment committees, amongst others. Additionally, at each table, each student has a role, including: table leader, materials manager, spokesperson, clerk, time controller, etc.

(4) **Evaluation:** This model takes into account the fact that students learn at different rates. Therefore, by being divided into subgroups (each classroom is usually made of 30 students), the teacher can identify the students who require more support in order to give them more attention. This also allows the students who are more advanced to continue and complement what has been learned with additional subjects. The evaluation scheme has a similar dynamic as well, where the teacher can evaluate the students once they reach the proposed challenges (activities or goals that should be completed in the different subjects – textbooks – or tasks). At this point it is necessary to clarify that the model has had to use approximation of measures of social and emotional competences, and this is an area of evaluation that needs work and strengthening.

(5) **School-family and community relationship**: Connections to families and the community are a fundamental aspect of the model, since we have to start from the reality that the schools are not islands, isolated from their larger community context. Students are part of a social structure that cares for them and that also needs them. The model includes different strategies to bring the community closer to school, for example there is a tool called the "Travelling notebook", which the students take home and parents should propose learning activities to be shared with all the classmates the day after. Other good example is that all the topics of the self-learning textbooks end with an "Application activity", which is meant to relate the theoretical approach with real life, so in this type of activities children should ask their parents to discuss with them this kind of relations.

(6) **Training for work:** In addition to developing cognitive, social, and emotional skills, the model promotes general work and entrepreneurship competencies, and has brought the university closer to school by providing technical (vocational) training programs parallel to usual secondary education during grades 10 and 11. As a result, the students leave eleventh grade with a technical degree that can give them the opportunity for 60% more income than if they left with just a secondary diploma.

The Active Urban Schools model has been implemented in the official schools of Manizales thanks to the aforementioned alliance and to a permanent strategy of formation and accompaniment with teachers and teaching directors throughout the city. Today, it has been implemented in 50% of the official schools of the city, which in general have shown very positive results (rural schools have the Escuela Nueva model, so most schools in the city already have an active pedagogical model).

A way forward

Above, I have explained in general the 21st century education that we want to promote and what we are specifically doing with one particular approach in Manizales, the Active Urban Schools model. The next step is to reflect on one of the possible paths to scale it, that we analyzed during the think tank, which contains the following steps organized chronologically, but with a wide spectrum of overlaps between them:

(1) **Political and social will for 21st century skills:** We need to spread, promote, expand, etc. the recognition of the need to make changes to educational institutions in favor of 21st century skills. Everything around us has been changing (our transportation systems, global communications, health services, international business, etc.), it should not be the case that our education remains the same as it was a few centuries ago. Students today require cognitive, interpersonal, and intrapersonal skills, and this must be clearly understood by our political and social leaders. The academic sector has a great responsibility here and should strive to bolster research and studies in these matters, ensuring that the message reaches the political sector. We must continue to strive in order that academic research moves from being solely in libraries and meetings between academics to being in the hands of political and social leaders.

(2) **Curriculum, understanding, and common goals**: The skills needed for the 21st century should be explicit in the curriculum, standards, and programs, and, most importantly, there must be a common understanding of what they include. It is not enough to have a taxonomy like the one by Pellegrino and Hilton that I previously presented. It is vitally important to clearly understand what each competence is looking for and how it has been conceived. Also, it is necessary to have common goals, built in a participatory way, between the private, public, and academic sectors—where I'm not only referring to universities, but also to teachers in schools, who are the first ones to want the best for their students. Teachers are the most capable to bring about these changes; but at the same time, they are also the ones who

91

have to do the hardest work to do. The must bring about real transformation at the classroom level, trying to impact students who have different needs, points of view, contexts, while in turn answering to diverse demands of school-level, city, country, and even global educational leadership stakeholders.

(3) **Training and accompaniment:** The proposed strategy should be tied to teacher training and development plans, which should always take into account teachers' pre-existing knowledge, and should respect their existing pedagogical processes. Training should also be considered apart from the "pre-service" (initial) training of the teachers.

(4) **Evaluation:** While the evaluation of skills is not the main issue, it is one of the most difficult and necessary to tackle. It is well known that what is not measured, cannot be improved. If we do not have a clear understanding of the skills, and how students are progressing or regressing in the acquisition of them, it will be very difficult to achieve the goals we have for 21st century education programs.

(5) **Interpret and analyze the results:** It is important to have analyzed and interpreted results, so that they reflect the observed reality in a way that is easily understood by others. This measurement should lead to for improvement efforts, as I mentioned before.

(6) **Reports and socialization:** How information is presented is key to the success of the strategy. The information collected must serve as input for working with teachers, and not to destroy or discourage the educational community. The group discussed the possibility of rankings, something that has many positive aspects, but can also have negative connotations. The rankings can often lead to unhelpful competition; however they frequently move leaders to action, because for they do not want to appear in lower places of the league tables.

(7) **Feedback and coaching for teachers:** This point is key since the results of evaluation should serve to refine the already mentioned training and development plans for teachers.

In this brief letter, I wanted to share my reflections on the skills needed for the 21st century, our experience with Active Urban Schools in

Manizales, and some general thoughts to take into account at the moment of wanting to scale transformative educational initiatives.

Santiago Isaza (Colombia), has been the Education and Project Manager at Luker Foundation in Manizales, Colombia, for more than 12 years, leading innovative initiatives in quality of education improvement, labor insertion, entrepreneurship, scientific interventions, education research, among others. He is an Industrial Engineer, with postgraduate studies in Project Management, International Business Management, Coaching and a Master degree in Prospective and Strategic Thinking. Is also teacher at the Universidad Externado of Colombia, in Knowledge Management in the Master of Education Quality Insurance and Measurement.

References

Pellegrino, J. W., & Hilton, M. L. (2012). Education for life and work: Developing transferable knowledge and skills in the 21st century. Washington, DC: The National Academies Press.

Scaling Up 21st Century Education: Reflections from Singapore

Pak Tee Ng, Associate Dean, Leadership Learning
National Institute of Education, Nanyang Technological University, Singapore

21st Century Competencies in Singapore

All schools in Singapore try to develop 21st century competencies (21CC) in their students, as part of the strategic direction of the Ministry of Education (MOE). Such competencies are critical to young people to help them address the demands of the 21st century society and workplace. These competencies can include knowledge of world issues and current affairs; literacy in terms of numerical, linguistic, cultural, scientific, and technological skills; lifelong learning skills; and the ability to manage novel situations and communicate new ideas. These changes take time to effectively permeate through the system as they are being implemented in the areas of curriculum, pedagogy, and assessment across all schools. MOE's 21CC Framework was developed to serve as a guide for teachers and school leaders to inculcate 21CC in their students across the educational spectrum.

"Scaling up" 21CC in Singapore

One of the main discussions during the GEII think tank was the challenge of scaling up the implementation of efforts to develop 21st century skills in young people in different jurisdictions. The assumption is that the efforts to develop 21st century skills in young people are local by some schools or organizations, and the question is how the reach of such efforts can be increased. However, as Singapore is a small country, 21CC is a national imperative that *all* schools implement. This approach creates synergy among schools through the sharing of experiences with one another, while allowing local-level variation in implementation to suit the profile of the students in the school. Therefore, Singapore's understanding and experience of scaling may be different from other education systems.

In Singapore, all schools have started to incorporate 21CC into their academic curriculum by refining their pedagogy and assessment, with many new skills and values being explicitly taught. While there are some 21CCs that are naturally inherent in the learning outcomes of certain subjects, others are cultivated through activities outside classrooms. One example is the use of co-curricular activities (CCAs) as a means of developing 21CC in students. Though CCAs have always existed in all Singapore schools, every school now emphasizes more explicit inculcation of 21CC through CCAs. CCAs are authentic platforms for the development of 21CC because they provide the perfect context for the learning and expression of moral values, the acquisition and practice of soft skills, and the social integration of children from different backgrounds and ethnic groups.

To support 21CC implementation, several national-level initiatives, such as the Programme for Active Learning (PAL), have been established across all Singapore schools. PAL was introduced into primary schools (Grades 1–6) to facilitate the all-round development of students and to provide varied avenues for students to develop social and emotional competencies through a broad range of experiences in sports, performing, and visual arts.

Challenges

The Singapore education system faces two main challenges in implementing 21CC. Firstly, the implementation is not totally even. It depends on the readiness of the school, teachers, parents, and community. For an education system that has been content-heavy and reliant on teacher-dominated pedagogies until the more recent years, not all teachers possess the necessary skills to meet the challenges posed to them with regards to 21CC teaching. Therefore, professional development, training, and retraining have been important. Schools also need to effectively engage stakeholders—parents, the community, industry and other training institutions—with the 21CC implementation, as they cannot embark on the 21CC journey alone. A strong relationship with stakeholders is critical to support the building up a child in 21CC. The reality is that some schools are more successful in implementation than others.

Secondly, Singapore still needs to put a lot of effort in helping stakeholders to change their mindsets regarding what successful education is. Singapore's system has traditionally been one that is preoccupied with grades, and the large and still-growing outside-of-school tuition industry clearly shows that parents want their children to excel academically. This results-oriented mindset poses a challenge for schools that would like to innovate, as parents still hold schools accountable for their child's performance in the national examinations. Only with a shift of focus from an acquisition of grades to an acquisition of life skills, and a change of mindset among educators, parents, and community alike, can 21CC be fully implemented. This of course will be a long journey.

Strength of Singapore System

The strength of the Singapore system is precisely its *system-ness*. Important education policies and initiatives are implemented at the national level, with autonomy given to school for local adaptation. With a common purpose, schools and practitioners are given top-down support for bottom-up initiatives to achieve the aims of 21st century education. The education system meets schools where they are and helps them implement policies sensibly and meaningfully. Progress cannot be rushed. Effective implementation is better than rushing into eventual failure.

The Singapore education system relies on its consistent alignment of policies, preparation, and practices in order to succeed. In implementing and sustaining continual efforts at improving and teaching 21CC, a strategic collaboration between policy-makers, teacher-educators, and school practitioners provides the platform for a united purpose and shared goals. Each partner plays a distinct role. But they work in harmony to achieve the desired outcomes of 21CC. This gives Singapore an edge in implementing 21st century education on a national scale.

Pak Tee Ng is Associate Dean, Leadership Learning at the National Institute of Education, Nanyang Technological University, Singapore. He teaches in executive programmes for school leaders (Principal-ship and Head-of-Department-ship), postgraduate programmes for research candidates (Master, EdD and PhD), and foundation programmes for trainee teachers. Pak Tee's main areas of teaching, research, training and consultancy are Educational Leadership, Educational Policies, Learning Organisation, Change Management, Knowledge Management,

Innovation, Complexity, and Coaching. His latest book, published by Routledge, is *Learning from Singapore: The Power of Paradoxes.*

Acknowledgements: I would like to thank Janey Ng and Jarrod Tam for helping me with drafts of this reflection.

Implications to develop 21st century skills with the use of technology in public schools in Mexico: UNETE's experience

Alejandro Almazan Zimerman, Chief Executive Officer of UNETE
Cesar Alberto Loeza Altamirano, Education Director of UNETE

Public K-12 education in Mexico is underachieving, to say the least. Its flaws are underpinned by four main setbacks: poor quality, lack of equity, insufficient coverage, and high dropout rates. All of them make public education unattractive and share at least one common element: the teaching and learning processes have not evolved at the same pace as society. This disparity between the official education discourse and the need to develop pertinent knowledge, skills, and competencies in order to integrate students as productive members of society has a negative impact on the country's competitiveness. So, what can be done to deliver an education that can improve students' achievement and provide them with the tools necessary to flourish in a changing world? This open letter makes the case that UNETE is attempting to (at least partially) address this problem. The information presented in this essay does not aspire to be comprehensive, but aims to enrich the Global Education Innovation Initiative's (GEII) conversation on how to promote and scale 21st century education in a sensible way.

UNETE[10] is an award-winning nonprofit with the objective of improving quality and equity of education in Mexico by means of developing a set of 21st century skills through the proper use of technology in public schools. Every school year, more than 2.5 million students across the whole country have access to media labs installed by UNETE, reaching more than 12% of the Mexican primary and secondary population. The organization has aided over 100,000 teachers and trained more than 30,000 educators on digital literacy.

Throughout UNETE's seventeen years of experience, its intervention model has evolved with a trial-and-error mindset. Initially, the organization's main focus was on providing underserved schools with access to technology. Today, its value proposition is centered on developing certain 21st century skills among teachers and students with

---

[10] www.unete.org

the use of technology. This shift, however, has not been an easy endeavor and it is still work in progress.

Barriers to promoting 21st century skills

First of all, the concept of 21st century skills is not commonly used nor *understood* across Mexico. Although skills such as collaboration, critical thinking, creativity, and communication (commonly referred to as the four C's) are employed on a frequent basis in the education sector, teachers and policy makers are not inclined to appreciate them as they probably should. There is a broad theoretical framework that supports the importance to develop them in students, but the concept is mostly used among niche audiences.

This lack of appreciation has a direct impact on what the authorities expect from the *curriculum*. Around the year 2012, the Mexican government introduced the concept of competencies in the official syllabus. Teachers were supposed to have a cross-sectional approach to their classes in order to develop certain competencies. However, what really happened in the field is that teachers did not fully understood the concept of competencies, their completion depended on inputs outside their taught classes, and the assessment of these competencies wasn't clear. Hence, this effort was not embraced by the school community. Taking this failed experience as a reference, aspiring to have the 21st century skills as an additional outcome in the official curriculum might receive strong resistance from the education community again.

Assessing 21st century skills is paramount to scale. Whatever you cannot define, you cannot measure. If you cannot measure, you cannot control. If you cannot control, you cannot improve. If you cannot improve, it will eventually deteriorate and eventually, fail. Thus, another barrier to promoting 21st century skills is the need for an accessible and intuitive way to evaluate them. A practical process that teachers can compare, report on, and use to make pedagogical improvements is vital. Otherwise, any proposal will be no more than wishful thinking.

Teachers are known to have a strong vocation to educate and to become mentoring figures for their students. Nevertheless, they also happen to be *incentive*-driven human beings with individual goals and personal ambitions. Consequently, any proposal to develop 21st century skills should be accompanied by a set of smart incentives that can motivate teachers to embrace the competencies and to promote their development in students. Since the education sector has had the same academic performance measures for decades (maths, reading, and writing), transitioning to a different approach will require creativity and reliability from an incentive perspective.

Finally, public schools in Mexico live an *underprivileged* reality. The common practice held among them to cope with basic repairs, maintenance, and general overhaul costs is through voluntary payments by the parent community. Under those conditions, education priorities need to compete against conditions such as no running water, broken toilets, constant class interruptions for political reasons, and clashes between teachers and parents. It would be naïve to assume that these grassroots problems don't impact the learning outcomes and would not interfere with schools' ability to dedicate time and effort to develop 21st century skills.

Practices that have worked for UNETE to develop 21st century skills with the use of technology

UNETE started equipping media labs with a very intuitive approach rather than following any specific *theoretical framework*. As time went by, new components to the model were introduced, such as training teachers on their digital skills. However, it wasn't until UNETE joined an international effort from the OECD called "Innovative Learning Environments," which outlined key principles of a 21st century education, that UNETE started to support schools in a more clearly articulated way. This milestone led to the adoption of other methodologies for the organization, some of which were eventually customized to the Mexican reality and embraced by its stakeholders.

UNETE's support model for schools is implemented with a *systemic approach*. In addition to equipping media labs with technology and connectivity, the organization trains teachers on their digital proficiency, shares educational content through the computers, solves technical and pedagogical questions with a help desk, provides additional tools and content through an educational portal, provides individualized support for teachers, and assesses the impact of the entire model. It wasn't until UNETE started to concern itself more with the skills-related outcomes on attributable to the supports it provides than about the output of equipping schools, that different components of the model became relevant as interrelated services. The organization soon realized that the synergy generated by such integrality was mandatory to aspire to develop teachers' and students' skills.

One of the biggest obstacles to scaling initiatives nationwide is linked to *funding* limitations. The way in which UNETE has managed to build a national footprint is with a multi-sector funding model. On the one hand, the organization has a set of donor allies that support every school UNETE equips. These organizations are Nacional Monte de Piedad, the most prestigious pawnshop in the country; Fundacion Televisa, the philanthropic arm of a multimedia mass media company; and BECALOS, a charitable vehicle from the Mexican Bank Association and Microsoft. In addition to those companies, UNETE asks the community itself to fund part of the project. The community pays for part of their training expenses, classroom refurbishments, and the costs of strengthening security measures at school. In this way, the school community becomes part of the solution and ends up appreciating the project differently. Finally, implementing the model requires the leadership of a main donor. These social investors can range from the government at its different levels (federal, state, or municipal), private companies, foundations, international donors, individuals, and so forth. As funding spreads across different stakeholders, the chances of success increase.

Any project aiming to impact teachers in schools should be appealing to them. Hence, in order to engage teachers, methodologies should ideally comply with three main success factors: (i) be practical, (ii) address teachers' needs; and (iii) be easy to understand. If these conditions are met, it will be easier to *empower* teachers with the use of technology. As they become more comfortable introducing technology into their teaching, it becomes easier to propose new collaborative projects promoting research, teamwork, community impact, and feedback to improve the outcomes. As students become more familiar with technological tools, then they too will be able to make use of their creativity, collaboration, communication, and critical thinking skills to solve particular academic problems.

In order to verify whether the organization is delivering its value proposition with success, it needs to receive constant *feedback*. This feedback should be transformed into knowledge, and the knowledge must lead to decision making. The first type of feedback is linked to the impact generated on beneficiaries. In that sense, UNETE hires independent evaluators to assess a statistically significant set of schools to understand what happened in terms of learning outcomes in teachers and students. The second type of information comes from analyzing the operating indicators with a business intelligence perspective to frequently monitor how the program execution unfolded. These evaluation practices are important for shaping the organizational culture in order to make sure that UNETE is fulfilling its purpose.

Unsolved questions and dilemmas

Throughout the years, there has been a set of conundrums to which there were no clear-cut answers. The ways in which those challenges were dealt with have been in response to specific circumstances. Nevertheless, all of these challenges and solutions contribute to the broader discussion on the implications of scaling 21st century skills. There is no doubt that UNETE benefits as a member of the GEII by learning how similar organizations and actors solved issues such as the following:

(1) A *"one size fits all"* approach does not take specific contexts into account, reducing the program's efficacy. However, a completely customized approach makes it difficult to run programs in an efficient way. So, where should the right balance be placed? At what cost?

(2) The *equity vs efficiency* dilemma has not been resolved yet. Under a reality with limited available resources, UNETE's support should ideally go to schools with better conditions to take advantage of the model. Nonetheless, the government has proven not to be reliable to improve the conditions of schools in remote places. Those children should have similar opportunities as the rest of the children in the country, and the development of their 21st century skills matters too. What should be the most appropriate allocation of resources?

(3) It is safe to say that the longer period of *time* UNETE supports a school, the higher the chances of impacting the school dynamics. As teachers familiarize themselves with the use of technology, they will feel more comfortable using it as a pedagogical tool for impacting students' learning processes. However, how much support time for teachers is needed to achieve irreversible results in engaging schools in the use of technology? Where is the tipping point? Is that tipping point short enough to make the model economically feasible?

(4) The main reason UNETE's value proposition is primarily centered around targeting teachers is to be able to leave a legacy in its work in schools and make the change *sustainable* after the organization leaves the school. If the support was given directly to children, schools would always depend on the organization. Yet, what does it take to engage the school community in full? Is it possible to make UNETE's support self-sustainable throughout time once the nonprofit leaves? What other stakeholders should be invited to the process to increase the depth of the impact?

(5) Worrying about the quality and equity of the education sector through the development of 21ˢᵗ century skills is a rewarding activity. Literally thousands of new lives are improved every year thanks to the philanthropic drive of a group of businessmen. But whose responsibility should it be? Isn't it the *government's duty* to improve the education system for all citizens? Aren't taxes justified to achieve goals like proper education for everyone? Are efforts similar to that of UNETE enough to tackle funding and programmatic shortfalls?

Harvard's leadership role in bringing together initiatives from around the world to promote 21ˢᵗ century skills is necessary to clarify concepts, learn from others, align efforts, customize solutions, and engage policy makers. As each initiative grows in reach and depth, our common aim to equip the coming generations with the necessary skills to become productive members of society at their own pace will have a positive impact on their communities and will increase their overall global competitiveness. A more prepared society will lead to a better world.

Alejandro Almazan Zimerman is CEO of UNETE, an NGO promoting the development of digital skills across Mexico. Previous to that role, he served the Mexican Government in the UK as a diplomat promoting trade and investment and also worked as a banker for Citigroup and as a financier for MRP, a private equity. Alejandro studied an MSc in Local Economic Development at the London School of Economics and a BA in Financial Management at the Monterrey Institute of Technology.

Cesar Alberto Loeza Altamirano is the Director of Education of UNETE.

Introducing 21ˢᵗ Century Skills in Brazil: Conecturma, Our Journey has Begun!

Rafael C. P. Parente, Chief Executive Officer, Aondê
with *Allan J. Coutinho, Ed.M. Student, Harvard Graduate School of Education*

In early October, 2016, I had the pleasure to attend a conference at the Harvard Graduate School of Education with other educational leaders from every corner of the world—leaders who are working to advance 21ˢᵗ century learning and who are serving children through innovative and transformative means. As someone who has contributed to similar efforts in Brazil, I was extremely pleased to contribute to this work and share my experiences as a former public official and the current CEO of Aondê, an organization that aims to boost literacy and, most importantly, introduce 21ˢᵗ century skills into the curriculum in schools across Brazil.

Co-authored with HGSE Ed.M student Allan J. Coutinho, this chapter briefly describes some of the systemic issues confronting children, teachers, and school leaders of Brazil, which have prevented the country from becoming a high performing system and delivering quality education, including 21st century skills. Second, this letter highlights what Conecturma does: How it aims to address some of these systemic issues, increase performance, and provide a framework for 21ˢᵗ century skills. Finally, this letter explores some of the strategies that our organization has been using to overcome challenges and scale up in our country. It concludes with some key lessons for leaders who may try to implement similar projects in their systems.

Brazil: Failing to deliver on its promise of (quality) education for all

Brazil's educational system is extremely deficient and plagued by social and regional disparities. Official evaluations show that less than two out of ten seventeen-year-old Brazilian teenagers know what they should in math and language (Indicadores da Educação, n.d.). However, this learning deficit starts early in life: more than half of all eight-year-olds in the country are not able to complete a simple numerical calculation (MEC divulga dados da ANA 2014, 2015).

These calamitous results are a product of myriad factors. Science has shown that one's intellectual and cognitive capability and the quality and depth of one's learning, depend on factors both internal and external to educational systems (Hattie, 2009). First, in order to build an understanding of the internal causes for poor performance, let us look at what happens within an average public school in Brazil—learning about what the daily lives of ordinary students, professors, and school leaders in these learning environments—and then we will comment on the factors external to the education system.

In general, Brazilian schools' equipment, infrastructure, curriculum, routines, and pedagogical strategies are outdated. Schools' interior and exterior spaces are neither inspiring nor welcoming. Many students feel they are in hostile places and that they are not part of a community. Moreover, they may feel that the content that they learn will not help them acquire the 21st century skills needed to solve local and global issues and meet the ever changing demands of highly specialized labor markets (Torres, 2012). In these schools, the teaching methods differ completely from those applied in high performing systems, where new technologies, the internet, project-based learning, personalization, and gamification are a part of common pedagogy, innovational practices, and professional learning for teachers (da Silva & da Silva, 2014). In these schools, discoveries about learning from the field of neuroscience do not influence pedagogical action, and essential life skills and abilities are excluded from the learning goals.

As one of the most important school inputs that drives learning in schools, teachers need to be better equipped to change the status-quo. Teachers are not villains. They do not intend to create stressful routines or plan to become inefficient professionals. From my experience working in the educational sector in Brazil, I can tell that teachers are, in general, idealistic people who feel unmotivated to drive change due to the complex challenges that one can encounter in hard-to-staff classrooms and inadequate incentives (Conceição & Sousa, 2012). When the teaching profession is not attractive and initial education and professional development are insufficient, it becomes quite difficult to expect exceptional outcomes from educators.

Finally, we need to take into consideration the role that school leaders, superintendents, and other system leaders play as part of internal factors leading to poor performance. Locally, the selection of our leaders and principals are usually based on processes that do not favor leadership characteristics and management skills (Lück, 2014), which leads to underqualified applicants taking on challenges that they are not prepared to face or even provide the support that teachers need.

At the macro level, Brazil has more than 5,000 secretaries of education—educational leaders that rarely come to learn about high performing and international best practices and management models (Farenzena & Marchand, 2014). Locally and nationally, public policy suffers from implementation problems and the paucity of clear articulation among key human capital areas such as health, culture, and social assistance (Ferreira, Moysés, França, Carvalho, & Moysés, 2014). At all levels, the bureaucracy and the laws that govern public management inhibit innovation while political discontinuity exerts additional negative effects on teams, cultures, and processes (Couto, n.d.).

Externally, we know that school communities are made up of other stakeholders and that learning may happen anytime and anywhere. Differences in familial participation in a child's educational life are perceptible even before preschool—when the development of neural connections is so important (Becker, 2011). The number of words a child comes to learn in initial years has a huge impact on his future academic success, since the more we know, the easier it gets for us to learn new things (Willingham, 2009).

Nevertheless, in the Brazilian context, there is very little integration among schools, families, and neighborhoods. The socio-economic status of families, the little academic and vocabulary knowledge parents possess, as well as the social calamities affecting basically all communities across Brazil such as crime and violence, hinder learning in schools (Rosa, 2013).

I have noticed that people become discouraged in attempting to address these issues because these problems are so complex and too entrenched both internally and externally at all levels of the system. In my experience, I noticed that it becomes extremely difficult for people to think about innovative solutions, new pedagogies, and 21st century skills when an outdated and ineffective structure is so pervasive, especially when a system cannot even provide minimal levels of cognitive skills.

However, in the meantime, millions of children and teenagers lose the prospect of a better future in our schools. This leads to traumatic consequences in areas as diverse as health, social mobility, and peace. Most importantly, this inertia makes Brazil fail its children and future generations in making them to become empowered citizens of our economy and democracy. One thing is clear to me: We can no longer afford to prevent our children in schools from achieving the democratic principles of equality and justice that should unite us all as Brazilians and citizens of the world.

As I move forward with my plan to transform education in Brazil, I wonder how much talent we have to sacrifice in order for us to act and to promote change. Part of my decision to establish Conecturma and advocate for 21st century skills is based on the vision that children, regardless of their background, have the *right* to acquire the cognitive, intrapersonal, and interpersonal competencies that enable people to thrive and lead their lives successfully and peacefully in this world. The next section will explore the theory of change for Conecturma and how this project plans to make tangible contributions to this field.

Conecturma: Leading for the advancement of 21st century skills

Because the issues that make up the status quo seem intractable, my team decided to focus our attention on the literacy cycle and find entry points for change at this level. Our decision was based on two factors: First, in the primary literacy cycle alone, the problems in the Brazilian educational system undermine the learning experience of approximately five million Brazilian children. The deficiencies in cognitive skills at the end of this cycle preclude children's ability to perform well in the later stages of their academic lives (Gatti, da Silva, & Esposito, 2013).

These statistics created a sense of urgency that has driven our organization since day one. Once
we had defined our problem, we moved forward to learn and explore two of its most important subcases:

(1) Brazilian textbooks and teaching methodologies have not been fundamentally changed over the decades to align with international best practices, so they do not incorporate technological developments or new discoveries in the fields of neuroscience and pedagogy (Martins, 2016).

(2) Brazilian teachers do not have adequate initial education nor professional development; they do not have access to quality resources and are unmotivated (Veiga, da Silva, Xavier, & de Arruda Fernandes, 2015).

Our organization is aiming to change this reality by providing teachers with appropriate resources for quality education and 21st century skills. Our goal is to increase the performance of students on the official evaluations by 30% and to develop all of the following human dimensions: innovation, adaptability, leadership, entrepreneurship, collaboration, global citizenship, analysis and synthesis of information, communication, productivity, social responsibility, and critical thinking. Conecturma combines physical textbooks with an adaptive and gamified digital platform in order to maximize student engagement, concentration, and all of the competencies mentioned above. Different from current practice, we are trying to develop children's cognitive skills while giving the appropriate attention to the intrapersonal and interpersonal competencies that are necessary for global citizenship. This is an innovative methodology created by Aondê Educational, an EdTech startup based in Rio de Janeiro, which aims to provide a platform and the best learning experience to educate autonomous, compassionate, and competent citizens.

Aware of the challenges confronting teachers' initial and continued education, Conecturma gives these professionals modern tools and processes for their teaching. As a result, they are able to provide a more interactive, fun, and relevant educational experience for their students, which is confirmed by the feedback the organization receives from teachers, parents, and students. The content is flexible and can be implemented to suit the needs of different school systems, adapting to a wide range of infrastructures and pedagogical realities.

Since the very beginning of this initiative, we knew that we had to win teachers' hearts and minds if they were to embrace the new methodology and challenge their boundaries of knowledge. We were asking teachers to teach children 21st century skills and, at the same time, educate themselves about methodology. As part of the intervention, we created an "initial education" program so as to leverage teachers' prior knowledge with best practices. So, in addition to providing an innovative online platform and textbooks, our organization delivered training sessions to facilitate learning and gain teachers' buy in. When we engaged with teachers in these meetings, we reinforced the fact that they can create and innovate in their classrooms in parallel with Conecturma.

In order to further support teachers, we also utilized strategies to motivate these educators and respond to their inquiries, regardless of the locality they serve in Brazil. Learning from the experience of other international development projects and industries across the world, we began to map how these teachers could communicate effectively with us. Despite the structural challenges of some rural regions, we knew that the vast majority of teachers had access to cell phones and the WhatsApp communications app. We utilized this app, together with a strategic planning process for the entire school community, to enhance our communication and implementation plan. Moreover, we delivered souvenirs with our contact information, puppets that represented Conecturma's children's cartoon characters, and other materials to optimize the utilization of our resources.

Since 2015, Conecturma has been used to teach Portuguese, mathematics, and socio-emotional skills to students in different Brazilian regions, in both public and private school networks. In 2015, 1,000 students were taught with Conecturma. In 2016, the quantity was doubled to 2,000 and Aondê aims to include 8,000 students by 2017. The company's goal for the next five years is to reach 300,000+ elementary school students countrywide and to help these students improve their cognitive skills—besides the pivotal intrapersonal and interpersonal capabilities needed for global citizenship.

Challenges and Lessons from Conecturma

We have learned a great deal during our implementation cycle. Needless to say, this is true for any project. In an environment as challenging and diverse as ours, one has to be able to learn and adapt if one truly wants to reach to the most vulnerable children and hard-to-staff schools. Despite our careful mapping and strategic planning, we have come across the following hurdles:

- Poor infrastructure in schools, including supply of old computers and lack of new ones and internet connection.
- Teachers' demotivation to innovate due to their lack of experience with technology.
- Ideological bias against our pedagogical materials as people believe that structured resources may hinder teachers' creativity.

We initiated Conecturma knowing about the structural challenges of our schools. However, it did not prevent us from acting and implementing a program that enforces 21st century skills. Again, we act on the premise that *someone* has to take the initial step forward. More than an organization, we have to become a powerful voice and advocate for structural improvements in schools in order to scale up nationwide. As a result, part of our strategic planning involves mapping out relevant stakeholders and engaging with partners, foundations, and organizations that can help us enforce this agenda and mobilize public and private funds toward this pivotal cause. Organizations do not operate alone and we came to learn this very quickly doing this type of work in Brazil.

From this experience, we also learned that the greatest threat for innovation is what happens when ideas are not aligned to the context which they try to transform. Since the very beginning, we knew that capacity constraints would be a challenge for the implementation of Conecturma. It does not matter if an organization can develop a product based on best practices if capacity is inexistent or insufficient. Our organization becomes less efficient in the delivery of its promise of quality education if schools do not provide minimal levels of technology and internet to its students and teachers. Therefore, part of our work has included advocacy and capacity building for the system as we implement and scale up Conecturma.

Secondly, despite our marketing, outreach, and initial educational initiatives to empower teachers, Conecturma still faces some resistance from some educators. Our organization has witnessed in-service teachers with very little computing literacy skills learning about new technologies and transforming their pedagogy. Nevertheless, a few have continued to challenge the project due to fear, and have stated that structured teaching materials hinder their capacity for innovation.

However, one can argue the opposite. Because Brazil is still on track to becoming a high performing system and still possesses very little teaching capacity (Bruns & Luque, 2014), we believe that organizations like ours have to *support* teachers and provide guidelines upon which they can improve their work and become even more innovative. In fact, Conecturma is far from dictating which practices teachers have to use in classrooms; rather, it provides a framework for change and facilitates a dialogue on the matter, always emphasizing the contributions that it can make to students' development.

Our experience with Conecturma has demonstrated that many teachers embrace this theory of action. Conecturma has taught us that organizations must make countless efforts to send a clear message to its clients regarding their products and methods. It also reinforced the idea that marketing and outreach initiatives are an endless endeavor for new organizations.

These are some of the initial learnings from our organization that we contribute in this book. We have shared our initial experiences and lessons from implementing Conecturma, and we hope that you come to learn more about this type of collective experiential learning from other organizations that advance 21st century skills globally in this book too.

To conclude, we would like to send a message of hope. Brazil has a long way to go before it empowers *all* of its children and youth to become real global citizens. We have listed some of the issues confronting the Brazilian educational system and described how the inertia has harmed the prospects of a better future for our children. Looking at large systems with similar problems, one can become discouraged from acting. However, we are certain that for every problem, there certainly are multiple opportunities and entry points for change. We call upon partners working on spreading 21st century skills across the world—who share the vision that all children have the right to receive good quality education—to act with their communities, find

114

entry points, and create space for change. We need more action, learning, and engagement if we truly aspire to build a sustainable and exciting future for ourselves and for our children.

Rafael Parente is PhD in education (NYU), CEO of an edtech start-up (Aondê / Conecturma), president of the council of CEIPE and associate of the Movement Todos pela Educação. He was the founder and director of LABi (Laboratory of Educational Innovation) - 2014-2017 - and the deputy secretary of education of Rio de Janeiro - 2009 to 2013. With his team, he created and implemented highly successful policies such as Educopédia, Rioeduca, and GENTE.

Allan J. Coutinho is a Lemann Fellow and an Ed.M student in the International Education Policy Program at Harvard Graduate School of Education. Prior to Harvard, Allan participated in several international education experiences through the U.S. Department of States -- as a Youth Ambassador of Brazil and United States Achievers Program Fellow -- and through the Japanese Ministry of Education, as a Japanese Jasso Scholar. Allan collaborates with CEIPE as a policy analyst.

References

Becker, B. (2011). Social disparities in children's vocabulary in early childhood. Does pre-school education help to close the gap?. *The British journal of sociology, 62*(1), 69–88.

Bruns, B., & Luque, J. (2014*). Great teachers: How to raise student learning in Latin America and the Caribbean.* World Bank. Retrieved February 3, 2016 from https://openknowledge.worldbank.org/handle/10986/20488

Conceição, C., & Sousa, Ó. D. (2012). Ser professor hoje: O que pensam os professores das suas competências. *Revista Lusófona de educação,* (20), 81–98.

Couto, J. D. (n.d.). DESCONTINUIDADE DAS AÇÕES PÚBLICAS EM EDUCAÇÃO. Retrieved November 8, 2016 from   http://www.anped.org.br/sites/default/files/poster-gt05-3650.pdf.

da Silva, A. L., & da Silva, P. M. (2014). Práticas avaliativas e aprendizagens significativas em diferentes áreas do currículo. *Temática*, *9*(3), XX–XX.

Farenzena, N., & Marchand, P. S. (2014). Relações intergovernamentais na educação à luz do conceito de regulação. *Cadernos de Pesquisa*, *43*(150), 788–811.

Ferreira, I. D. R. C., Moysés, S. J., França, B. H. S., Carvalho, M. L., & Moysés, S. T. (2014). Percepções de gestores locais sobre a intersetorialidade no Programa Saúde na Escola. *Revista Brasileira de Educação*, *19*(56), 61–76.

Gatti, B. A., da Silva, R. N., & Esposito, Y. L. (2013). Alfabetização e educação básica no Brasil. *Cadernos de Pesquisa*, (75), 7–14.

Hattie, J. (2009). *Visible learning: A synthesis of over 800 meta-analyses relating to achievement.* London: Routledge.

Indicadores da Educação. (n.d.). Retrieved November 7, 2016 from http://www.todospelaeducacao.org.br/indicadores-da-educacao/5-metas?task=indicador_educacao&id_indicador=15#filtros

Lück, H. (2014). Mapeamento de práticas de seleção e capacitação de diretores escolares. *Relatório Final. Centro de Desenvolvimento Humano Aplicado (Cedhap).*

Martins, I. (2016). Analisando livros didáticos na perspectiva dos Estudos do Discurso: compartilhando reflexões e sugerindo uma agenda para a pesquisa. *Pro-posições*, *17*(1), 117–136.

MEC divulga dados da ANA 2014. (2015, September 25). Retrieved November 8, 2016, from http://www.todospelaeducacao.org.br/reportagens-tpe/35337/mec-divulga-dados-da-ana-2014/

116

Rosa, M. J. A. (2013). Violência no ambiente escolar: refletindo sobre as consequências para o processo ensino aprendizagem. *Revista Fórum Identidades*.

Torres, H. G. (2012). O que pensam os jovens de baixa renda sobre a escola. Retrieved November 8, 2016 from http://www.fvc.org.br/estudos-e-pesquisas/2012/pensam-jovens-baixa-renda-escola-743754.shtml

Veiga, I. P. A., da Silva, E. F., Xavier, O. S., & de Arruda Fernandes, R. C. (2015). A didática na formação docente: entre a inovação técnica e a edificante. *III EDIPE–Encontro Estadual de Didática e Prática de Ensino-2009*. Retrieved November 8, 2016 from http://www.ceped.ueg.br/anais/IIIedipe/pdfs/2_trabalhos/gt09_didatica_praticas_ensino_estagio/trab_gt09_a_didatica_na_formacao_docente. pdf

Willingham, D. T. (2009). *Why don't students like school: A cognitive scientist answers questions about how the mind works and what it means for the classroom*. John Wiley & Sons.

Made in the USA
Columbia, SC
13 April 2018